Icebox Pies

Also by Lauren Chattman:

COOL KITCHEN

JUST ADD WATER

INSTANT GRATIFICATION

MOM'S BIG BOOK OF BAKING

Icebox Pies

100 *Scrumptious Recipes for*

No-Bake No-Fail Pies

LAUREN CHATTMAN

The Harvard Common Press, Boston, Massachusetts

For Alexandra, *pastry-chef-in-training*

THE HARVARD COMMON PRESS
535 Albany Street
Boston, Massachusetts 02118
www.harvardcommonpress.com

Printed in China
Printed on acid-free paper

Library of Congress Cataloging-in-Publication Data
Chattman, Lauren.
   Icebox pies : 100 scrumptious recipes for no-bake, no-fail pies / Lauren Chattman.
      p. cm.
      Includes index.
   ISBN 1-55832-212-4 (cl : alk. paper) -- ISBN 1-55832-213-2 (pb : alk. paper)
      1. Pies. 2. Cookery (Cold dishes) I. Title.
   TX773.C473 2002
   641.8'15—dc21

                                                                              2001051537

Special bulk-order discounts are available on this and other Harvard Common Press books.
Companies and organizations may purchase books for premiums or resale, or may arrange a
custom edition, by contacting the Marketing Director at the address above.

10   9   8   7   6   5   4   3   2

Cover and interior design by Night & Day Design
Photographs by Duane Winfield
Food styling by Nir Adar
Prop styling by Robyn Glaser

Acknowledgments

It was Pam Hoenig's idea to do a book on icebox pies; I just ran with it. I'd like to thank everyone else at The Harvard Common Press for their devotion to the subject: Bruce Shaw, Valerie Cimino, Skye Stewart, Christine Alaimo, Abbey Phalen, Sunshine Erickson, Georgina Duff, Virginia Downes, and Jodi Marchowsky. It was a pleasure to work with copyeditor Maggie Carr again. Duane Winfield's photos are simply beautiful, and I thank Justin Schwartz for helping with them. Suzanne Heiser's design is as fresh as these pies. Thanks as always to Angela Miller, agent and good friend. Yvette Willock was always willing to taste and critique. And thanks to Jack, Rose, and Eve, who were always ready to try another pie.

Contents

Introduction *Discovering Icebox Pies*

One day when I was finishing up a book about baking, my editor called and asked if I'd like to write a book on icebox pies. Not one to turn down work, I said, "Sure." Only after I hung up did I realize that I had no idea what an icebox pie was.

Like most people, I always assumed that pies came from the oven. You roll out some dough, fit it into a pie pan, fill it with fruit, and bake it until it is bubbly, right? I had a vague notion of Key lime pie, although I had never tasted one. In my travels I had seen chocolate cream pie a number of times at truck stops and diners, but I had never dared to order a slice. At home, it had always been strictly apple, pumpkin, pecan, and blueberry—all pies that depend on the heat of the oven to transform the basic ingredients into dessert.

As soon as I started to think about the subject, I got excited. After a quick look at a few recipes for icebox classics like grasshopper pie and black bottom butterscotch pie, the concept felt familiar and comfortable. For these pies, you didn't have to roll out any dough. The fillings were either uncooked or made in a pot on the stove. They were easy.

My first book, *Cool Kitchen*, was filled with recipes that didn't require actual cooking. My second book, *Just Add Water*, was for people whose only kitchen skill was the ability to bring liquid to a boil. Next, I wrote *Instant Gratification*, a collection of 15-minute desserts. Most recently, I tried with *Mom's Big Book of Baking* to perfect and simplify all of the recipes an ideal mother would have. Yet here was a category of simple, no-bake, stovetop desserts that I had completely overlooked. I had been handed a perfect opportunity to discover a whole new way to make dessert without a whole lot of work.

I loved the idea, and once I started experimenting, I loved the desserts. The terms "icebox" and "pie" conjured up visions of quaint desserts from the past. Indeed, the pies in this book have a nostalgic flavor. They are beautiful and special, but at the same time they are too simple and homey to be mistaken for the sophisticated, complicated desserts you see in restaurants today. I wanted to create pies that would look and taste just like something your mother or grandmother would have made if she had been a very, very good cook. Make my Triple Chocolate Mint Pie and I promise you will be able to imagine yourself sitting in an old-fashioned kitchen, maybe at an enamel-topped table, enjoying a slice fresh from the icebox with a tall, frosty glass of milk while your apron-clad granny looks on with satisfaction.

The reality is that you don't have to be a domestic goddess or fantasy grandmother to make these desserts. Icebox pies might seem old-fashioned, but because they are easy to put together and can be made well in advance of serving, they are perfect for contemporary cooks who crave nostalgic indulgences but don't have a lot of time or much kitchen experience. The crust for that Triple Chocolate Mint Pie consists of Oreo cookies pulverized in a food processor and mixed with a little melted butter. The filling is a simple but rich chocolate pudding that comes together on the stove in less than 10 minutes. You can make the pie up to a day in advance of serving. When you're ready to be transported back to that imaginary kitchen, all you have to do is slice the pie and pour the milk.

Icebox Pie Defined

Before I began this project in earnest, I wanted to come up with a definition of icebox pie that would be flexible enough to include a wide variety of desserts for many tastes and occasions, but still precise enough to signify something. I didn't want "icebox pie" to mean just any old pie that's spent some time in the refrigerator. Here is what I settled on:

- Icebox pies have cookie-crumb crusts that are easy to make and that remain crisp even after being filled with moist ingredients and refrigerated for hours. Crumb crusts do need a little time in the oven to crisp up, six to eight minutes to be exact. This is the only baking that any of these pies requires. The crusts may be made ahead of time and frozen until you are ready to use them.
- The fillings are either uncooked or cooked on top of the stove. None of them need to be baked. There are no meringue or brûlé toppings that require heating in the broiler.
- Once the fillings have been transferred to the crumb crusts, these icebox pies must spend a minimum of three hours in the refrigerator or freezer so that the filling can set completely. The refrigerator or freezer is not just a place to store an icebox pie. Chilling the pie actually finishes the cooking process.

Chapter 1, on crumb crusts, will give you a range of crusts using different kinds of cookie crumbs that work with the wide variety of icebox pies in this book. The subsequent chapters feature different types of icebox pies.

Chapter 2 contains recipes for mousse, pudding, and custard pies. These desserts can be as down-home as Marshmallow Pie (it's just what it sounds like) or as refined as Frozen Prune Mousse Pie. If it's a creamy filling in a crumb crust, it's here.

Chapter 3 has icebox pies for chocolate fans. This is where you will find Chocolate Pudding Pie, along with Rocky Road Pie, White Chocolate and Raspberry Pie, Chocolate and Honey Pudding Pie, Milk Chocolate and Cherry Pie, and a dozen others.

Chapter 4 is the place to go if you like fruit and cream combinations. Each pie in this chapter consists of three elements: a crisp crumb crust, a creamy filling, and a fruit topping. The recipes range from whipped cream topped with kiwis to mascarpone studded with cherries to rich rice pudding slathered with rhubarb jam.

Chapter 5 details the various ways to

use store-bought ice cream, frozen yogurt, and sorbet to make the simplest frozen pies. Of course, there are plenty of kid-friendly desserts here. You can pick up the ingredients for Peanut Butter Cup Pie at your local convenience store—my children's favorite place to shop for snacks. Trail Mix Pie is chockablock with yummy mix-ins that children love: peanuts, chocolate chips, raisins, coconut. There are also some surprisingly grown-up desserts for casual entertaining. Pistachio and Orange Ice Cream Pie, served with Warm White Chocolate Sauce, is a wonderfully simple way to end a summer dinner party.

I call **Chapter 6** "I Can't Believe It's an Icebox Pie," because this is the place where I've collected icebox recipes that taste like "real" baked pies. Check out the ultra-simple Blueberry Icebox Pie with a cornstarch-thickened stovetop filling, or the Chocolate-Almond Icebox Pie that's as satisfying as any nut pie that comes out of the oven.

Finally, in **Chapter 7**, I've gathered together all of the toppings and accompaniments I use to dress up the pies in the earlier chapters. Here you'll find recipes for Coffee Whipped Cream, Chocolate Coconut Sauce, Sugared Nuts, and a whole lot of other add-ons for icebox pies.

Into the Icebox

The one thing that each of these recipes has in common is the icebox part. Every single pie must be refrigerated or frozen before it will be ready to be served. In the case of these pies, the icebox is not just for storage. Chilling or freezing the pie allows the filling to thicken and set, giving it the proper consistency for serving. The refrigerator or freezer is to the icebox pie as the oven is to any baked pie. You wouldn't think of eating your Thanksgiving Day pumpkin pie before it's been baked. Don't think about cutting into your Pumpkin Mousse Pie before it has been well chilled.

Chilling times vary from recipe to recipe, but most pies require at least three hours in the refrigerator or freezer to set up. Refrigerated pies can usually be stored for up to one day before the crust begins to get soggy (exceptions are noted throughout). Frozen pies, wrapped tightly in plastic, stay good in the freezer for a week with no diminishment of quality.

Each recipe has specific instructions for wrapping and storing. In general, pies should be tightly covered in plastic wrap. Not only does plastic prevent the surface of the pie from drying out or developing unappetizing "pudding skin"; it also prevents the pie from absorbing any odors wafting around in your refrigerator. The last thing you want to add to your icebox pie is a subtle hint of pickle juice or leftover meatloaf. Pay special attention to frozen pies when covering them in plastic, since they may be sitting in the freezer for a long time. A tight wrapping will save frozen pies from freezer burn, which is unsightly and tastes awful.

Out of the Icebox and onto the Table

When dinner is done and the dishes have been cleared, it's time to prepare the pie for serving. If it's been frozen, let it sit on the counter for 10 or 15 minutes to soften up. If it's been refrigerated, you may slice it immediately.

After slicing countless icebox pies many different ways with varying results, I've developed a two-implement technique for transferring neat slices to dessert plates. First I'll use a sharp paring knife to cut through the filling and crust. Then I'll carefully insert a pointy-tipped metal cake server underneath the slice and lift it from the pie pan. Sometimes it's tough to get the first piece out without losing a bit of the crust, but subsequent pieces are a breeze to serve if you're using the paring knife to cut and the cake server to lift.

I usually garnish an icebox pie with extra toppings and sauces after slicing the pieces and putting them on plates. I like the way individual slices look, all dressed up like sundaes. And I find that it's less messy to put a dollop of whipped cream on each slice than to slather whipped cream across the whole pie and then slice the cream-covered pie. Depending on how casual the service is at your house, you may either top each slice yourself after taking requests or just put the accompaniments out and let everyone top his or her own.

If one of your guests doesn't want whipped cream or is allergic to nuts, this saves that person the inconvenience and embarrassment of having to scrape the unwanted accompaniments to the side of the plate.

I'm one of those cooks who is always afraid that I won't have enough food, and who inevitably has a week's worth of leftovers after a dinner party. I suggest in the recipes that each pie will serve six to eight people. But if your guests are already pretty full from dinner, you will probably get a couple more servings out of a pie, especially if it is particularly rich or if you are serving it with a couple of accompaniments.

Essential Ingredients for Icebox Pie

A successful icebox pie consists of a crisp crumb crust and a flavorful filling that's been thickened enough and allowed to set long enough so that the pie may be cut into more or less neat slices. The process is simple, but you need the right ingredients to produce such a dessert. Fortunately, these ingredients are neither exotic nor difficult to work with. Most are familiar pantry and refrigerator staples. All are available in any supermarket.

It may be stating the obvious, but it's always worth repeating: Quality ingredients are essential for making a quality dessert. The techniques, such as they are, for making great icebox pies are easily mastered, but if the ingredients are inferior, your pie will be substandard, too. Cheap chocolate, bad fruit, or nuts that have been sitting around for too long on the supermarket or pantry shelf will adversely affect your finished pie. Buy the freshest, best items available. Your reward will be a delightful dessert.

Here is a list of the things I frequently use to make icebox pies, with some tips on buying and storing them.

Butter: Butter is essential for making the tastiest and crispest crumb crusts. I always use unsalted butter and add just a pinch of salt to the crumb mixture for flavor. Butter will keep for at least a month in the freezer, so I stock up when there's a sale.

Chocolate: When I plan to make a chocolate icebox pie, I always buy a premium brand of chocolate such as Lindt or Ghirardelli, rather than inexpensive semisweet baking squares. Not surprisingly, expensive chocolate gives pies a richer flavor and a smoother texture. I like Dutch-process unsweetened cocoa. Pernigotti, available at Williams-Sonoma, is my favorite brand. I keep bags of mini chocolate chips on hand (regular chocolate chips are too bulky to use in icebox pies) to mix into crumb crusts and a variety of fillings.

Cookie crumbs and cookies: Pre-ground graham cracker crumbs taste just as good as the crumbs you crush yourself, and they are a great convenience. Since I have two small children, I usually have boxes of Oreos, vanilla wafers, gingersnaps, and zwieback cookies around for spur-of-the-moment pie making.

Cornstarch: Cornstarch is an excellent, easy-to-use thickener that gives pudding and fruit fillings a glossy shine and smooth texture. To prevent lumps from forming, you'll need to dissolve the cornstarch in cold water before you add it to a filling mixture.

Eggs: Eggs thicken and enrich a variety of icebox pie fillings. All of the recipes in this book have been tested with large eggs. Usually, I heat eggs to a safe temperature of 160 degrees when preparing egg-based fillings. But there are a few recipes in this book that call for raw eggs. Because of the remote but dangerous possibility that raw eggs carry salmonella, they should not be used in food to be consumed by children, pregnant women, elderly people, or anyone in poor health or with a compromised immune system. When appropriate, I mention that dried egg whites may be substituted for fresh ones.

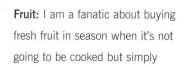

Fruit: I am a fanatic about buying fresh fruit in season when it's not going to be cooked but simply arranged on top of an icebox pie filling. For cooked fruit fillings, I will use individually quick frozen (IQF) fruit if fresh isn't available. Whether or not frozen fruit may be substituted for fresh fruit is noted in individual recipes.

Gelatin: Flavorless gelatin turns liquids into semisolids and is essential for many mousse fillings. It comes packaged in individual packets of powder and must be dissolved in a liquid and then gently heated before being added to the rest of the filling ingredients.

Heavy cream: If you ever see pasteurized (not ultra-pasteurized) organic heavy cream in your market, buy it! It whips up lighter and tastes fresher than regular ultra-pasteurized cream. But all of the recipes in this book work just fine with the much more common ultra-pasteurized cream.

Ice cream: Ice cream, frozen yogurt, and sorbet are among the simplest fillings for icebox pie. Unless I'm broke, I buy luxury brands of ice cream with high butterfat content. The richer the ice cream, the better the pie. If you're watching fat and calories, quality brands of lowfat frozen yogurt or nonfat sorbet are good alternatives with a lot of flavor.

Liqueurs and spirits: Kahlua, Grand Marnier, Kirsch, framboise, dark rum, brandy, and other liqueurs and spirits add depth to icebox pies. I keep small bottles around to use in desserts. Use alcohol sparingly, however. Too much of it will prevent whipped cream fillings from obtaining maximum volume and will prevent gelatin-based fillings from gelling.

Nuts: Nuts add welcome crunch to icebox pies. I stir them into crumbs for crust, or use them in toppings. Nuts are expensive and go bad quickly, but I go through a lot of them. I buy large bags of nuts from my local warehouse club and then store the nuts in airtight containers in the freezer to preserve freshness.

Essential Equipment for Icebox Pie
You will need just a few basic pieces of kitchen equipment to make an icebox pie. The refrigerator and freezer are the big-ticket items, but I assume you already possess them if you've picked up this book. The other items are standard in most kitchens, but I've included a few buying recommendations if you are still in the market for one or two.

Double boiler: A double boiler creates a gentle heat that melts chocolate so that it is smooth and not grainy. It heats eggs slowly enough so they won't curdle. It is also handy for melting gelatin. If you don't own a double boiler, you can improvise by placing a metal bowl over a saucepan filled with an inch or two of simmering water.

Electric mixer: I use a heavy duty Kitchen-Aid mixer. There's nothing like it for whipping cream or egg whites. But such a powerful machine is not necessary for whipping together icebox pie filling. A handheld mixer is more than adequate, although it might take a few seconds longer.

Food processor: This is an essential piece of equipment for making cookie crumbs, chopping nuts, and puréeing fruit. I have an 11-cup-capacity Cuisinart model, but a smaller food processor is just fine.

Measuring cups and spoons: Successful icebox pies depend on precise proportions of ingredients. Measure accurately and carefully with glass or clear plastic "liquid" measuring cups for liquid ingredients and plastic or metal "dry" measuring cups for large quantities of dry ingredients. For small quantities, use measuring spoons. Fill cups and spoons completely and level off ingredients with a knife for accurate measurements.

Mixing bowls: It's good to have mixing bowls in all sizes, not only for mixing together fillings but for organizing ingredients before you start to cook. I buy inexpensive sets of stainless-steel and glass bowls that nest together for easy storage.

Paring knife: A sharp paring knife is a must for preparing many types of fruit. More important, the pointy top and sharp edge are perfect for cutting neat slices of pie before lifting them from the pie pan with a pie server or spatula. Buy a flexible but strong knife with an extra-sharp edge. Premium brands like Wüsthof and Henckels will last a lifetime and are well worth the relatively high price.

Pie pans: All of the recipes in this book call for a 9-inch pie pan. I prefer glass pans because they bake crumb crusts evenly, but if you already have metal pans they will work fine.

Pie server: This utensil is essential for lifting slices neatly from the pie pan after they have been cut.

Spatulas: It's helpful to have a couple of rubber spatulas for scraping fillings from mixing bowls into pans. A metal offset spatula comes in handy for smoothing filling once it's in the shell.

Strainer: I like to pour certain fillings such as lemon, orange, or lime curd through a fine strainer to make sure that they are perfectly smooth. It's convenient if the strainer has a little metal loop opposite its long handle; that way you can rest the strainer on the bowl and use two hands to pour and scrape the filling into the strainer. Individual recipes contain specific instructions on when it's a good idea to strain a filling.

Wire whisks: A whisk will break up lumps that a mere spoon will miss. This is a necessary item if you want smooth, not lumpy, fillings.

No Rolling Pin Required *Simple Crumb Crusts*

Graham Cracker Crust

Graham Cracker and Nut Crust

Graham Cracker and Coconut Crust

Graham Cracker and Chocolate
Chip Crust

Graham Cracker and Oatmeal
Crumb Crust

Chocolate Cookie Crust

Chocolate Cookie and Nut Crust

Oreo Cookie Crust

Gingersnap Crust

Zwieback Crust

Vanilla Wafer Crust

Vanilla Wafer and Sliced
Almond Crust

Amaretti Crust

Lemon Nut Cookie Crust

Sugar Cone Crust

As a professional pastry chef and avid home baker, I've mixed and rolled my share of pie dough. But no matter how many times I do it, I can never shake the anxiety that grips me every step of the way. Sometimes I worry that I've added too little water; sometimes I worry that I've added too much. Will I wind up with a tough crust because I've handled the dough too roughly? Have I stretched the dough while placing it in the pan, so that it will shrink when it goes into the oven? Have I blind-baked it long enough, or will the bottom become wet and gluey as the pie sits and cools?

In contrast, I make crumb crusts absolutely fearlessly and in no time at all. There is nothing scary about putting some cookies in the workbowl of a food processor and pulverizing them, stirring in a little sugar and melted butter, and pressing the mixture into a pie pan. Using your fingers this way feels like playing; in fact, pressing crumbs into a pan is so simple that if you've had any sandbox experience as a child, you'll be able to do it flawlessly on your first try.

Not only are they quicker and easier than pastry crusts; crumb crusts make better icebox pies. While a pastry crust will become soggy if filled and refrigerated overnight, a crumb crust will stay crisp and continue to serve as a sturdy base. Crumb crusts are wonderfully versatile. Whether you are making Chocolate Pudding Pie, Papaya Mousse Pie, or Strawberry Cheesecake Pie, there's a crust that will bring out the best in the filling.

Varying the flavor of the crust is as simple as choosing a different box of cookies. First among equals is the graham cracker crust. With its unobtrusive flavor and wonderful texture, a pie crust made of graham cracker crumbs will complement almost any filling. You may tailor a graham cracker crust to a specific filling by adding ground nuts, flaked

coconut, miniature chocolate chips, or rolled oats. Crusts made with packaged graham cracker crumbs taste the same as crusts made with home-ground crumbs, so I usually save time and use the packaged variety. In this chapter, I include recipes for all kinds of graham cracker crusts, as well as recipes for crusts made with chocolate wafer cookies, Oreos, zwieback cookies, gingersnaps, vanilla wafers, amaretti, and Pepperidge Farm Lemon Nut Cookies. Different kinds of cookies need different amounts of butter and sugar, but the basic technique, if you can call it that, is the same for every crust.

Alongside each recipe throughout the rest of the chapters in this book I've included my crust choices. But these are only suggestions. Use any of the following crust recipes in any of the pie recipes, according to your own taste.

A few words about "technique": For a crust that holds together and slices easily, make sure to pat the cookie mixture into the pan firmly, so that there are no loose crumbs. Pat the crumbs all the way up the sides of the pie pan, or your shell might not be able to hold all of the filling.

Crumb crusts for icebox pies must be baked so that they don't fall apart. Be careful, however, not to overbake the crust. Six to eight minutes is more than enough to solidify the crumb mixture. Any longer than this and your crust might become too hard and might even begin to shrink down the sides of the pan as it loses moisture.

Make sure to cool the crust completely before you fill it. Cooling the crust allows it to crisp up and stay crisp until serving time. A warm crust may ruin delicate fillings. If you pour a whipped cream mixture into a warm crust, the filling will deflate. For obvious reasons, you don't want to put ice cream into a hot pie shell.

Once they are baked and cooled, crumb crusts can be wrapped in plastic and frozen for up to a month. If you are making a frozen pie or an ice cream pie, you may use the frozen crust directly from the freezer. If you are making a pie that will be refrigerated, defrost the crust overnight in the refrigerator before filling it.

Graham Cracker Crust

Makes one 9-inch pie crust

This classic crumb crust bakes up crisp and not too sweet—perfect for almost any icebox pie.

11 whole graham crackers (to yield about 1⅓ cups crumbs)

5 tablespoons unsalted butter, melted

1 tablespoon sugar

⅛ teaspoon salt

1. Preheat the oven to 350 degrees.

2. Place the graham crackers in the workbowl of a food processor and process them until they are finely ground. Combine the crumbs, butter, sugar, and salt in a medium-size mixing bowl and stir until the crumbs are moistened.

3. Press the mixture evenly across the bottom of a 9-inch pie plate and all the way up the sides of the pan, packing it tightly with your fingertips so it is even and compacted.

4. Bake the crust until it is crisp, 6 to 8 minutes. Let it cool completely before filling it. (The crust may be wrapped in plastic wrap and frozen for up to 1 month.)

Graham Cracker and Nut Crust

Makes one 9-inch pie crust

Ground nuts add flavor and richness to a basic graham cracker crust. Select the type of nut that you think will taste best with your filling.

11 whole graham crackers (to yield about 1⅓ cups crumbs)

½ cup pecans, walnuts, almonds, or skinned hazelnuts (page 50)

¼ cup (½ stick) unsalted butter, melted and slightly cooled

1 tablespoon sugar

⅛ teaspoon salt

1. Preheat the oven to 350 degrees.

2. Place the graham crackers and nuts in the workbowl of a food processor and process them until they are finely ground. Combine the crumb-and-nut mixture, butter, sugar, and salt in a medium-size mixing bowl and stir until the crumb-and-nut mixture is moistened.

3. Press the mixture evenly across the bottom of a 9-inch pie plate and all the way up the sides of the pan, packing it tightly with your fingertips so it is even and compacted.

4. Bake the crust until it is crisp, 6 to 8 minutes. Let it cool completely before filling it. (The crust may be wrapped in plastic wrap and frozen for up to 1 month.)

Graham Cracker and Coconut Crust

Makes one 9-inch pie crust

This is the obvious choice for any pie made with coconut milk or cream of coconut. It's also fabulous filled with chocolate pudding or vanilla ice cream.

11 whole graham crackers (to yield about 1⅓ cups crumbs)

¼ cup (½ stick) unsalted butter, melted

⅓ cup sweetened flaked coconut

1 teaspoon pure coconut extract

⅛ teaspoon salt

1. Preheat the oven to 350 degrees.

2. Place the graham crackers in the workbowl of a food processor and process them until they are finely ground. Combine the crumbs, butter, coconut, coconut extract, and salt in a medium-size mixing bowl and stir until the crumbs are moistened.

3. Press the mixture evenly across the bottom of a 9-inch pie plate and all the way up the sides of the pan, packing it tightly with your fingertips so it is even and compacted.

4. Bake the crust until it is crisp, 6 to 8 minutes. Let it cool completely before filling it. (The crust may be wrapped in plastic wrap and frozen for up to 1 month.)

Graham Cracker and Chocolate Chip Crust

Makes one 9-inch pie crust

This crust tastes like a chocolate chip cookie. The chocolate sweetens the crust, so it's not necessary to add any sugar. Be sure to cool the butter or the chips will melt.

11 whole graham crackers (to yield about 1⅓ cups crumbs)

5 tablespoons unsalted butter, melted and cooled

½ cup miniature semisweet chocolate chips

1 teaspoon pure vanilla extract

⅛ teaspoon salt

1. Preheat the oven to 350 degrees.

2. Place the graham crackers in the workbowl of a food processor and process them until they are finely ground. Combine the crumbs, butter, chocolate chips, vanilla, and salt in a medium-size mixing bowl and stir until the mixture is moistened.

3. Press the mixture evenly across the bottom of a 9-inch pie plate and all the way up the sides of the pan, packing it tightly with your fingertips so it is even and compacted.

4. Bake the crust until it is crisp, 6 to 8 minutes. Let it cool completely before filling it. (The crust may be wrapped in plastic wrap and frozen for up to 1 month.)

Graham Cracker and Oatmeal Crumb Crust

Makes one 9-inch pie crust

Oats stirred into graham cracker crumbs make this crust extra chewy with a wholesome flavor.

11 whole graham crackers (to yield about 1⅓ cups crumbs)

5 tablespoons unsalted butter, melted

½ cup old-fashioned (not quick-cooking) rolled oats

3 tablespoons firmly packed light brown sugar

1 teaspoon pure vanilla extract

⅛ teaspoon salt

1. Preheat the oven to 350 degrees.

2. Place the graham crackers in the workbowl of a food processor and process them until they are finely ground. Combine the crumbs, butter, oats, brown sugar, vanilla, and salt in a medium-size mixing bowl and stir until the mixture is moistened.

3. Press the mixture evenly across the bottom of a 9-inch pie plate and all the way up the sides of the pan, packing it tightly with your fingertips so it is even and compacted.

4. Bake the crust until it is crisp, 6 to 8 minutes. Let it cool completely before filling it. (The crust may be wrapped in plastic wrap and frozen for up to 1 month.)

Chocolate Cookie Crust

Makes one 9-inch pie crust

These dark chocolate cookies make a surprisingly rich-tasting crust for all kinds of chocolate and ice cream pies.

30 Nabisco Famous Chocolate Wafers (to yield about 1⅓ cups crumbs)

5 tablespoons unsalted butter, melted and slightly cooled

⅛ teaspoon salt

½ teaspoon pure vanilla extract

1. Preheat the oven to 350 degrees.

2. Place the cookies in the workbowl of a food processor and process them until they are finely ground. Combine the crumbs, butter, salt, and vanilla in a medium-size mixing bowl and stir until the crumbs are moistened.

3. Press the mixture evenly across the bottom of a 9-inch pie plate and all the way up the sides of the pan, packing it tightly with your fingertips so it is even and compacted.

4. Bake the crust until it is crisp, 6 to 8 minutes. Let it cool completely before filling it. (The crust may be wrapped in plastic wrap and frozen for up to 1 month.)

Chocolate Cookie and Nut Crust

Makes one 9-inch pie crust

Nuts add some crunch and even more richness to a basic chocolate cookie crust. Use less butter, since the ground nuts add fat.

22 Nabisco Famous Chocolate Wafers (to yield about 1 cup crumbs)

½ cup pecans, walnuts, almonds, or skinned hazelnuts (page 50)

¼ cup (½ stick) unsalted butter, melted and slightly cooled

1 tablespoon sugar

⅛ teaspoon salt

½ teaspoon pure vanilla extract

1. Preheat the oven to 350 degrees.

2. Place the cookies and nuts in the workbowl of a food processor and process them until they are finely ground. Combine the crumb-and-nut mixture, butter, sugar, salt, and vanilla in a medium-size mixing bowl and stir until the crumb-and-nut mixture is moistened.

3. Press the mixture evenly across the bottom of a 9-inch pie plate and all the way up the sides of the pan, packing it tightly with your fingertips so it is even and compacted.

4. Bake the crust until it is crisp, 6 to 8 minutes. Let it cool completely before filling it. (The crust may be wrapped in plastic wrap and frozen for up to 1 month.)

Oreo Cookie Crust

Makes one 9-inch pie crust

Sometimes chocolate wafer cookies can be hard to find. But Oreos are always available and make a crust that is sweeter than Chocolate Cookie Crust. Much less butter is needed in this recipe since the Oreo filling helps to moisten the crumbs. I especially like this crust with ice cream pies.

20 Oreo cookies (to yield about 1½ cups crumbs)

2½ tablespoons unsalted butter, melted and slightly cooled

⅛ teaspoon salt

½ teaspoon pure vanilla extract

1. Preheat the oven to 350 degrees.

2. Place the cookies in the workbowl of a food processor and process them until they are finely ground. Combine the crumbs, butter, salt, and vanilla in a medium-size mixing bowl and stir until the crumbs are moistened.

3. Press the mixture evenly across the bottom of a 9-inch pie plate and all the way up the sides of the pan, packing it tightly with your fingertips so it is even and compacted.

4. Bake the crust until it is crisp, 6 to 8 minutes. Let it cool completely before filling it. (The crust may be wrapped in plastic wrap and frozen for up to 1 month.)

Gingersnap Crust

Makes one 9-inch pie crust

Use this crust when you want to add a little spice to your icebox pie.

25 gingersnap cookies (to yield about 1⅓ cups crumbs)

5 tablespoons unsalted butter, melted and slightly cooled

¼ teaspoon ground cinnamon

⅛ teaspoon salt

1. Preheat the oven to 350 degrees.

2. Place the cookies in the workbowl of a food processor and process them until they are finely ground. Combine the crumbs, butter, cinnamon, and salt in a medium-size mixing bowl and stir until the crumbs are moistened.

3. Press the mixture evenly across the bottom of a 9-inch pie plate and all the way up the sides of the pan, packing it tightly with your fingertips so it is even and compacted.

4. Bake the crust until it is crisp, 6 to 8 minutes. Let it cool completely before filling it. (The crust may be wrapped in plastic wrap and frozen for up to 1 month.)

Zwieback Crust

Makes one 9-inch pie crust

This crust made from children's cookies has a hint of cinnamon but is milder than a crust made from gingersnaps.

One 7-ounce box zwieback toasts (to yield about 1½ cups crumbs)

5 tablespoons unsalted butter, melted

¼ cup sugar

⅛ teaspoon salt

1. Preheat the oven to 350 degrees.

2. Place the zwieback toasts in the workbowl of a food processor and process them until they are finely ground. Combine the crumbs, butter, sugar, and salt in a medium-size mixing bowl and stir until the crumbs are moistened.

3. Press the mixture evenly across the bottom of a 9-inch pie plate and all the way up the sides of the pan, packing it tightly with your fingertips so it is even and compacted.

4. Bake the crust until it is crisp, 6 to 8 minutes. Let it cool completely before filling it. (The crust may be wrapped in plastic wrap and frozen for up to 1 month.)

Vanilla Wafer Crust

Makes one 9-inch pie crust

This is a kid-pleasing crust that goes well with a variety of simple fillings.

50 vanilla wafer cookies (to yield about 1½ cups crumbs)

5 tablespoons unsalted butter, melted and slightly cooled

⅛ teaspoon salt

1 teaspoon pure vanilla extract

1. Preheat the oven to 350 degrees.

2. Place the cookies in the workbowl of a food processor and process them until they are finely ground. Combine the crumbs, butter, salt, and vanilla in a medium-size mixing bowl and stir until the crumbs are moistened.

3. Press the mixture evenly across the bottom of a 9-inch pie plate and all the way up the sides of the pan, packing it tightly with your fingertips so it is even and compacted.

4. Bake the crust until it is golden and crisp, 6 to 8 minutes. Let it cool completely before filling it. (The crust may be wrapped in plastic wrap and frozen for up to 1 month.)

Vanilla Wafer and Sliced Almond Crust

Makes one 9-inch pie crust

Thinly sliced almonds don't need to be chopped in the food processor. Just add them directly to the cookie crumbs to give a plain vanilla crust a little more character.

40 vanilla wafer cookies (to yield about 1¼ cups crumbs)

5 tablespoons unsalted butter, melted and slightly cooled

⅛ teaspoon salt

1 teaspoon pure vanilla extract

¼ cup sliced almonds

1. Preheat the oven to 350 degrees.

2. Place the cookies in the workbowl of a food processor and process them until they are finely ground. Combine the crumbs, butter, salt, vanilla, and sliced almonds in a medium-size mixing bowl and stir until the crumb-and-nut mixture is moistened.

3. Press the mixture evenly across the bottom of a 9-inch pie plate and all the way up the sides of the pan, packing it tightly with your fingertips so it is even and compacted.

4. Bake the crust until it is golden and crisp, 6 to 8 minutes. Let it cool completely before filling it. (The crust may be wrapped in plastic wrap and frozen for up to 1 month.)

Amaretti Crust

Makes one 9-inch pie crust

4 whole graham crackers (to yield about ½ cup crumbs)

24 amaretti cookies (to yield about 1 cup crumbs)

5 tablespoons unsalted butter, melted

½ teaspoon pure almond extract

⅛ teaspoon salt

Ground amaretti cookies, combined with a few graham crackers, make a wonderfully fragrant crust that is good with a variety of fruit and chocolate fillings.

1. Preheat the oven to 350 degrees.

2. Place the graham crackers and amaretti cookies in the workbowl of a food processor and process them until they are finely ground. Combine the crumbs, butter, almond extract, and salt in a medium-size mixing bowl and stir until the crumbs are moistened.

3. Press the mixture evenly across the bottom of a 9-inch pie plate and all the way up the sides of the pan, packing it tightly with your fingertips so it is even and compacted.

4. Bake the crust until it is crisp, 6 to 8 minutes. Let it cool completely before filling it. (The crust may be wrapped in plastic wrap and frozen for up to 1 month.)

Lemon Nut Cookie Crust

Makes one 9-inch pie crust

Pepperidge Farm Lemon Nut cookies make a fresh-tasting crust, especially when a little lemon zest is thrown in for added flavor.

20 Pepperidge Farm Lemon Nut Cookies (to yield about 1½ cups crumbs)

3 tablespoons unsalted butter, melted and slightly cooled

½ teaspoon grated lemon zest

⅛ teaspoon salt

1 teaspoon pure vanilla extract

1. Preheat the oven to 350 degrees.

2. Place the cookies in the workbowl of a food processor and process them until they are finely ground. Combine the crumbs, butter, lemon zest, salt, and vanilla in a medium-size mixing bowl and stir until the crumbs are moistened.

3. Press the mixture evenly across the bottom of a 9-inch pie plate and all the way up the sides of the pan, packing it tightly with your fingertips so it is even and compacted.

4. Bake the crust until it is golden and crisp, 6 to 8 minutes. Let it cool completely before filling it. (The crust may be wrapped in plastic wrap and frozen for up to 1 month.)

Sugar Cone Crust

Makes one 9-inch pie crust

Crushed sugar cones make a great crust for ice cream pies.

11 sugar cones (to yield about 1⅓ cups crumbs)

5 tablespoons unsalted butter, melted

2 tablespoons sugar

1. Preheat the oven to 350 degrees.

2. Place the sugar cones in the workbowl of a food processor and process them until they are finely ground. Combine the crumbs, butter, and sugar in a medium-size mixing bowl and stir until the crumbs are moistened.

3. Press the mixture evenly across the bottom of a 9-inch pie plate and all the way up the sides of the pan, packing it tightly with your fingertips so it is even and compacted.

4. Bake the crust until it is crisp, 6 to 8 minutes. Let it cool completely before filling it. (The crust may be wrapped in plastic wrap and frozen for up to 1 month.)

Cool and Creamy Mousse and Custard Pies

Before I started working on this book, I had a pretty limited idea of what "icebox pie" could mean. Maybe it was a no-bake pie with a Key lime or vanilla pudding filling, or maybe it was a pie shell filled with some ice cream and topped with whipped cream and hot fudge.

Only after I accepted the challenge of developing a hundred recipes did I realize how wide open the category of icebox pies is. Pumpkin purée, frozen papaya chunks, cranberries, you name it: If it can be turned into a custard, pudding, or mousse, it can be turned into a pie. Once I realized this, my work was easy. All I had to do was make a list of my favorite dessert flavors and ingredients and figure out the simplest and best way to turn each one into a luscious filling for any of a number of delicious crumb crusts. I hope you will be as amazed and delighted as I am with the variety of great desserts that fit this description.

The easiest mousse fillings consist of a flavoring ingredient folded together with whipped cream. For example, the filling for Peanut Butter Pie consists of simply some peanut butter folded into sweetened whipped cream. For whipped cream pies with the greatest volume, make sure your cream is thoroughly chilled before whipping, and be sure to handle it gently when folding it together with the rest of the filling ingredients so as not to deflate the mousse. If the rest of the filling is heavy (as is peanut butter), lighten the heavy mixture by stirring in about one quarter of the whipped cream before attempting to fold the rest of the filling into the cream.

One degree of difficulty higher than a mousse, stovetop custard makes a delicious filling when folded together with whipped cream. It's a simple equation. Lemon curd and whipped cream become Lemon Cream Pie. Egg-based custards can be tricky; they will curdle if overcooked. If your lemon curd gets a little lumpy in the pan, however, don't fret. To eliminate any bits of hard-cooked egg, just push the lemon curd through a fine sieve before letting it cool.

Gelatin may be added to filling ingredients to give a pie a firmer texture. Pies thickened with gelatin can easily be cut into clean slices that will hold their shape beautifully. If the idea of a pie made with gelatin sounds hopelessly retro to you, you haven't considered Sour Cream and Honey Mousse Pie or Apricot-Almond Mousse Pie. You'd be more likely to see these sophisticated desserts at a good restaurant than at the local diner, even though they are simple enough for any short-order cook to prepare. And every once in a while it's *fun* to make a retro dessert. Marshmallow Pie won't be appearing on the menu at any four-star restaurants, but it's still a thoroughly enjoyable treat for kids of all ages.

Gelatin, with its magical ability to turn liquids into solids, is an indispensable ingredient if you want to transform pineapple juice and cream of coconut into Piña Colada Pie. Gelatin is highly sensitive to temperature, a fact you should keep in mind when working with it. It should be softened with a quick soak in cool water before being melted over simmering water or by being stirred into a warm liquid. If it isn't softened before it is warmed, it may not gel properly; if it is heated too much, its gelling properties will be destroyed. When stirring warmed gelatin into a cool liquid, make sure to whisk it in quickly and thoroughly. If the melted gelatin is not completely incorporated into the other ingredients before it begins to gel, it will form unappetizing, gooey strands.

The chapter ends with three of my absolute favorite icebox pies: Frozen Cranberry Mousse Pie, Frozen Prune Mousse Pie, and Toasted Almond Semifreddo Pie. Whipped egg whites give the fillings wonderful body. They taste like homemade ice cream, but without any of the fuss. If egg safety is a concern, substitute egg white powder (available in the baking aisle of the supermarket) mixed with water, following the package directions for equivalent measures. These frozen pies have a practical advantage over pies that are refrigerated. Each can be made a week in advance of serving. They all make great desserts for special occasions, and they are especially good drizzled with a warm dessert sauce. For easy cutting, let the frozen pies stand at room temperature for 10 to 15 minutes, especially if they've been in the freezer for more than a day.

Lemon Cream Pie

Makes one 9-inch pie; 6 to 8 servings

I've always found lemon curd too sweet and heavy on its own. Folded into whipped cream, however, it makes a wonderful pie filling.

6 large eggs

¾ cup sugar

2 teaspoons grated lemon zest

¾ cup fresh lemon juice

½ cup (1 stick) unsalted butter, cut into 8 pieces

1 cup heavy cream, chilled

1 prepared crumb crust

1. Combine the eggs, sugar, and lemon zest in a heavy medium-size saucepan and whisk the mixture until it is smooth. Add the lemon juice and butter and cook the mixture over medium heat, whisking constantly, until it is thickened, 7 to 9 minutes. Do not allow the mixture to come to a boil.

2. Pour the lemon curd through a fine mesh strainer into a glass bowl. Cover the surface with plastic wrap. Refrigerate the lemon curd until it is cold and thick, at least 3 hours and up to 3 days.

3. In a medium-size mixing bowl using an electric mixer, whip the heavy cream until soft peaks form. Gently fold the whipped cream into the lemon curd and scrape the filling into the prepared pie shell. Cover the pie with plastic wrap and refrigerate it until the filling is completely set, at least 6 hours and up to 1 day.

CHOOSING A CRUST

My favorite crust for this pie is **Vanilla Wafer Crust** (page 17).

DRESSING IT UP

Spoon some **Raspberry Coulis** (page 131) onto dessert plates, place pieces of pie on top, and scatter kiwi slices on top of and around the slices of pie.

Peanut Butter Pie

Makes one 9-inch pie; 6 to 8 servings

*Although
I like peanut butter
on a sandwich, I like it
even better after it's been
folded into a luscious
whipped cream pie
filling.*

2½ cups heavy cream, chilled

¾ cup plus 2 tablespoons confectioners' sugar

2 teaspoons pure vanilla extract

1 cup smooth peanut butter

1 prepared crumb crust

4 ounces bittersweet chocolate, finely chopped

½ cup unsalted dry-roasted peanuts, finely chopped

1. Combine 2 cups of the cream, the sugar, and vanilla in a large mixing bowl and using an electric mixer beat the cream until stiff peaks form.

2. Place the peanut butter in a medium-size mixing bowl and stir in one quarter of the whipped cream. Gently fold the lightened peanut butter mixture back into the remaining whipped cream. Scrape the filling into the prepared pie shell, smooth the top with a rubber spatula, and refrigerate the pie until the filling is firm, about 3 hours.

3. Heat the remaining ½ cup heavy cream in a small saucepan until just boiling. Remove the pot from the heat and whisk in the chocolate until the mixture is smooth. Let the topping cool until it is just warm to the touch. Spread it over the chilled pie with a rubber spatula. Sprinkle on the chopped peanuts. Cover the pie with plastic wrap and refrigerate it until the filling is completely set, at least 3 hours and up to 1 day.

CHOOSING A CRUST

Graham Cracker Crust (page 11) is traditional; **Graham Cracker and Chocolate Chip Crust** (page 12), **Chocolate Cookie Crust** (page 13), and **Oreo Cookie Crust** (page 14) are fine substitutes.

DRESSING IT UP

Instead of spreading the melted chocolate topping over the pie, drizzle **Hot Fudge Sauce** (page 127) or **Chocolate Peanut Butter Sauce** (page 128) over slices of pie and top with dollops of whipped cream and the chopped peanuts.

Orange and Spice Pie

Makes one 9-inch pie; 6 to 8 servings

1. Combine the eggs, sugar, orange zest, ginger, and cardamom in a heavy medium-size saucepan and whisk the mixture until it is smooth. Add the orange juice and butter and cook the mixture over medium heat, whisking constantly, until it is thickened, 7 to 9 minutes. Do not allow the mixture to come to a boil.

2. Pour the orange curd through a fine mesh strainer into a glass bowl. Cover the surface with plastic wrap. Refrigerate the orange curd until it is cold and thick, at least 3 hours and up to 3 days.

3. In a medium-size mixing bowl using an electric mixer, whip the heavy cream until soft peaks form. Gently fold the whipped cream into the orange curd and scrape the filling into the prepared pie shell. Cover the pie with plastic wrap and refrigerate it until the filling is completely set, at least 6 hours and up to 1 day.

Cardamom gives orange curd an intriguing flavor.

6 large eggs

¾ cup sugar

2 tablespoons grated orange zest

1 teaspoon ground ginger

½ teaspoon ground cardamom

1 cup orange juice

½ cup (1 stick) unsalted butter, cut into 8 pieces

1 cup heavy cream, chilled

1 prepared crumb crust

CHOOSING A CRUST
I like plain **Vanilla Wafer Crust** (page 17), which doesn't interfere with the flavors of the pie.

DRESSING IT UP
Dollops of whipped cream with or without Grand Marnier are wonderful on slices of this pie. If you like, sprinkle some chopped crystallized ginger on top, too.

Marshmallow Pie

Makes one 9-inch pie; 6 to 8 servings

1 cup whole milk

4 cups miniature marshmallows
  (about 6½ ounces)

1 tablespoon unsalted butter

1 teaspoon pure vanilla extract

1 cup heavy cream, chilled

¾ cup unsalted dry-roasted peanuts,
  coarsely chopped

1 prepared crumb crust

Here is an easy pie with uncomplicated flavors. Marshmallows already contain gelatin, so there's no need to add any to the filling.

1. Combine the milk and marshmallows in a heavy medium-size saucepan and heat the mixture over medium-low heat, whisking often, until the marshmallows are melted and the mixture is smooth. Remove the pot from the heat and transfer the mixture to a stainless-steel bowl.

2. Stir in the butter and vanilla. Set the bowl over a larger bowl of ice water and let the mixture stand, whisking occasionally, until it has cooled and begun to thicken, 5 to 10 minutes.

3. In a medium-size mixing bowl using an electric mixer, whip the heavy cream until it holds soft peaks. Gently fold the whipped cream into the marshmallow mixture.

4. Scatter the peanuts across the bottom of the prepared pie crust. Scrape the marshmallow filling into the prepared pie shell. Cover the pie with plastic wrap and refrigerate it until the filling is completely set, at least 6 hours and up to 1 day.

CHOOSING A CRUST

Graham Cracker and Chocolate Chip Crust (page 12) is perfect here, as is plain **Graham Cracker Crust** (page 11).

DRESSING IT UP

Hot Fudge Sauce (page 127) or **Chocolate Peanut Butter Sauce** (page 128) would finish this pie nicely. Garnish each slice with a couple of miniature marshmallows or one large toasted marshmallow, if you like.

Pumpkin Mousse Pie

Makes one 9-inch pie; 6 to 8 servings

1. Place the water in a small stainless-steel bowl and sprinkle the gelatin over the water. Let the gelatin stand to dissolve.

2. Put 2 inches of water in a medium-size saucepan and bring it to a bare simmer. Whisk the egg yolks and sugar together in a medium-size stainless-steel bowl and place the bowl on top of the simmering water, making sure that the bottom of the bowl doesn't touch the water. Heat, whisking constantly, until the egg mixture registers 160 degrees on an instant-read thermometer.

3. Remove the bowl from the pan of water and whisk in the gelatin mixture. Using an electric mixer, beat the mixture until it is cool and thick, about 5 minutes. Beat in the pumpkin purée, cinnamon, ginger, cloves, and vanilla.

Although this pie has the same flavors as traditional Thanksgiving Day pumpkin pie, it has a lighter texture, thanks to the whipped cream folded into the filling.

4. In a medium-size mixing bowl using an electric mixer, whip the heavy cream until soft peaks form. Gently fold the whipped cream into the pumpkin mixture.

5. Scrape the filling into the prepared pie shell. Cover the pie with plastic wrap and refrigerate it until the filling is completely set, at least 6 hours and up to 1 day.

1 tablespoon cold water

1 teaspoon unflavored gelatin

3 large egg yolks

½ cup sugar

1 cup canned pumpkin purée

½ teaspoon ground cinnamon

½ teaspoon ground ginger

⅛ teaspoon ground cloves

½ teaspoon pure vanilla extract

1 cup heavy cream, chilled

1 prepared crumb crust

CHOOSING A CRUST
No question: **Gingersnap Crust** (page 16).

DRESSING IT UP
Whipped cream would be welcome, with or without **Maple Walnut Sauce** (page 130).

Cinnamon-Butterscotch Pudding Pie

Makes one 9-inch pie; 6 to 8 servings

6 tablespoons cornstarch

1 teaspoon ground cinnamon

3½ cups half-and-half

¼ cup (½ stick) unsalted butter

¾ cup firmly packed dark brown sugar

¼ teaspoon salt

1 prepared crumb crust

1. Combine the cornstarch, cinnamon, and ½ cup of the half-and-half in a small mixing bowl and whisk the mixture until it is smooth.

2. Combine the butter, brown sugar, and salt in a heavy medium-size saucepan and cook the mixture over low heat, whisking occasionally, until the butter is melted and the sugar is dissolved. Add the remaining 3 cups half-and-half and the cornstarch mixture and turn the heat to medium-high. Continue to cook the pudding, whisking constantly, until it thickens, 3 to 4 minutes.

3. Scrape the pudding into the prepared pie shell. Place plastic wrap directly on the surface of the filling and refrigerate the pie until the filling is completely set, at least 6 hours and up to 1 day.

A generous spoonful of cinnamon enlivens this butterscotch pudding pie.

CHOOSING A CRUST
Graham Cracker and Oatmeal Crumb Crust (page 13) makes this homey pie even more comforting. If you can never get enough spice, use a **Gingersnap Crust** (page 16) or a **Zwieback Crust** (page 16).

DRESSING IT UP
Whipped cream is nice but not necessary.

Frozen Maple Mousse Pie

Makes one 9-inch pie; 6 to 8 servings

1. Put 2 inches of water in a medium-size saucepan and bring the pot to a bare simmer. Whisk the egg yolks and maple syrup together in a medium-size stainless-steel bowl and place the bowl over the simmering water, making sure that the bottom of the bowl doesn't touch the water. Heat the egg-and-maple mixture, whisking constantly, until it registers 160 degrees on an instant-read thermometer.

2. Remove the bowl from the pan and using an electric mixer beat the egg-and-maple mixture until it is cool and thick, about 5 minutes. Stir in the rum.

3. In another medium-size mixing bowl using an electric mixer, whip the heavy cream until soft peaks form. Gently fold the whipped cream into the egg-and-maple mixture.

4. Scrape the filling into the prepared pie shell. Cover the pie with plastic wrap and refrigerate it until the filling is completely set, at least 6 hours and up to 1 day.

Use grade B (rather than the more expensive grade A) maple syrup for the most maple flavor.

4 large egg yolks

½ cup pure maple syrup

2 tablespoons dark rum

1⅓ cups heavy cream, chilled

1 prepared crumb crust

CHOOSING A CRUST

Graham Cracker Crust (page 11) or **Graham Cracker and Nut Crust** (page 11) is perfect.

DRESSING IT UP

Sugared Walnuts (page 132), coarsely chopped, may be gently pressed into the top of the pie just before serving or sprinkled over a topping of whipped cream.

Piña Colada Pie

Makes one 9-inch pie; 6 to 8 servings

2 tablespoons cold water

2 teaspoons unflavored gelatin

⅔ cup sugar

3 large eggs

One 6-ounce can pineapple juice

½ cup unsweetened coconut milk

¾ cup heavy cream, chilled

1 prepared crumb crust

The flavors of pineapple and coconut combine to make a scrumptious, summery pie.

1. Place the cold water in a small stainless-steel bowl and sprinkle the gelatin over the water. Let the gelatin stand to dissolve.

2. Put 2 inches of water in a medium-size saucepan and bring the pot to a bare simmer. Whisk the sugar, eggs, pineapple juice, and coconut milk together in a medium-size stainless-steel bowl and place the bowl on top of the simmering water, making sure that the bottom of the bowl doesn't touch the water. Heat, whisking constantly, until the mixture registers 160 degrees on an instant-read thermometer.

3. Remove the bowl from the pan of water and whisk in the gelatin mixture. Set the bowl over a larger bowl of ice cubes and let the pineapple mixture stand, whisking occasionally, until it has begun to thicken, about 10 minutes.

4. In a medium-size mixing bowl using an electric mixer, whip the heavy cream until it holds soft peaks. Gently fold the whipped cream into the pineapple mixture.

5. Scrape the filling into the prepared pie shell. Cover the pie with plastic wrap and refrigerate it until the filling is completely set, at least 6 hours and up to 1 day.

CHOOSING A CRUST

Vanilla Wafer Crust (page 17) is a good neutral background for these flavors.

DRESSING IT UP

Drizzle some **Mango Coulis** (page 131) over slices of pie. Garnish each serving with some fresh raspberries if you like.

Espresso Mousse Pie

Makes one 9-inch pie; 6 to 8 servings

2 tablespoons cold water

2 teaspoons unflavored gelatin

One 14-ounce can sweetened
  condensed milk

¼ cup instant espresso powder

2 cups heavy cream, chilled

1 prepared crumb crust

1. Place the cold water in a small stainless-steel bowl and sprinkle the gelatin on top. Let the gelatin stand to dissolve.

2. Combine the condensed milk, espresso powder, and ½ cup of the heavy cream in a heavy medium-size saucepan and bring the espresso mixture just to a boil, stirring occasionally. Remove the pot from the heat and whisk in the gelatin mixture. Transfer the contents to a stainless-steel bowl.

3. Set the stainless-steel bowl over a larger bowl of ice cubes and let the espresso mixture stand, whisking it occasionally, until it has begun to thicken, about 10 minutes.

4. In a medium-size mixing bowl using an electric mixer, whip the remaining 1½ cups heavy cream until it holds soft peaks. Gently fold the whipped cream into the espresso mixture.

5. Scrape the mousse into the prepared pie shell. Cover the pie with plastic wrap and refrigerate it until the filling is completely set, at least 6 hours and up to 1 day.

This is an especially quick pie, with just a few ingredients. Sweetened condensed milk and heavy cream make it a super-rich indulgence.

CHOOSING A CRUST

Chocolate Cookie Crust (page 13), **Graham Cracker Crust** (page 11), or **Graham Cracker and Coconut Crust** (page 12) works here.

DRESSING IT UP

With **Chocolate Cookie Crust**, I pour **Warm Chocolate Sauce** (page 126) over slices of pie. With **Graham Cracker and Coconut Crust**, I like **Chocolate Coconut Sauce** (page 129).

Coconut Cream Pie

Makes one 9-inch pie; 6 to 8 servings

This simple pie contains a triple dose of coconut, from coconut milk, cream of coconut, and sweetened flaked coconut.

1. Place the cold water in a small stainless-steel bowl and sprinkle the gelatin on top. Let the gelatin stand to dissolve.

2. Combine the coconut milk and cream of coconut in a heavy medium-size saucepan and bring just to a boil, stirring occasionally. Remove the pot from the heat and whisk in the gelatin mixture. Transfer the contents to a stainless-steel bowl. Set the stainless-steel bowl over a larger bowl of ice cubes and let the coconut mixture stand, whisking occasionally, until it has begun to thicken, about 20 minutes.

3. In a medium-size mixing bowl using an electric mixer, whip the heavy cream until it holds soft peaks. Gently fold the whipped cream into the coconut mixture.

4. Scrape the filling into the prepared pie shell. Cover the pie with plastic wrap and refrigerate it until the filling is completely set, at least 6 hours and up to 1 day.

5. Just before serving, sprinkle the toasted coconut over the top and press it lightly into the pie so that it will adhere.

3 tablespoons cold water

1 envelope unflavored gelatin

One 14-ounce can unsweetened coconut milk

One 15-ounce can cream of coconut, such as Coco Lopez

¾ cup heavy cream, chilled

1 prepared crumb crust

¾ cup sweetened flaked coconut, toasted (page 66)

CHOOSING A CRUST

Graham Cracker and Coconut Crust (page 12) is a natural choice, although **Chocolate Cookie Crust** (page 13) or **Oreo Cookie Crust** (page 14) takes this pie in another direction.

DRESSING IT UP

Mango Coulis (page 131) picks up on the tropical theme here. Diced mango may be spooned over slices of pie if you prefer. **Warm Chocolate Sauce** (page 126) or **Chocolate Coconut Sauce** (page 129) is a fine alternative if you've chosen a chocolate crust.

Banana Cream Pie

Makes one 9-inch pie; 6 to 8 servings

For the best banana cream pie, make sure your bananas are very ripe.

2 tablespoons cold water

2 teaspoons unflavored gelatin

3 large eggs

½ cup sugar

1 teaspoon pure vanilla extract

1½ very ripe medium-size bananas, peeled and mashed

1 cup heavy cream, chilled

1 prepared crumb crust

1. Place the cold water in a small stainless-steel bowl and sprinkle the gelatin over the water. Let the gelatin stand to dissolve.

2. Put 2 inches of water in a medium-size saucepan and bring the pot to a bare simmer. Whisk the eggs and sugar together in a medium-size stainless-steel bowl and place the bowl on top of the simmering water, making sure that the bottom of the bowl doesn't touch the water. Heat, whisking constantly, until the mixture registers 160 degrees on an instant-read thermometer.

3. Remove the bowl from the pan and whisk in the gelatin mixture. With an electric mixer beat the mixture until it is cool and thick, about 5 minutes. Stir in the vanilla and bananas.

4. In a medium-size mixing bowl using an electric mixer, whip the heavy cream until soft peaks form. Gently fold the whipped cream into the banana mixture.

5. Scrape the filling into the prepared pie shell. Cover the pie with plastic wrap and refrigerate it until the filling is completely set, at least 6 hours and up to 1 day.

CHOOSING A CRUST
Graham Cracker and Coconut Crust (page 12) provides a crisp and sturdy base for the soft filling.

DRESSING IT UP
Drizzle pieces of pie with rum-flavored **Caramel Sauce** (page 129); garnish with slices of banana.

Sour Cream and Honey Mousse Pie

Makes one 9-inch pie; 6 to 8 servings

1. Place the cold water in a small bowl and sprinkle the gelatin on top. Let the gelatin stand to dissolve. Whisk together the sour cream and honey in a medium-size mixing bowl.

2. Put 1 inch of water in a small saucepan and bring the pot to a bare simmer. Place the bowl containing the gelatin on top of the simmering water and heat the gelatin, whisking constantly, just until it melts, 30 seconds to 1 minute. Whisk the gelatin mixture into the sour cream mixture until the consistency is smooth.

3. In a large mixing bowl using an electric mixer, whip the heavy cream until it holds soft peaks. Gently fold the sour cream mixture into the whipped cream.

Not only does honey sweeten this pie; it gives it a lovely flavor as well.

4. Scrape the filling into the prepared pie shell. Cover the pie with plastic wrap and refrigerate it until the filling is completely set, at least 6 hours and up to 1 day.

5. When you are ready to serve the pie, preheat the oven to 350 degrees. Place the sliced almonds on a baking sheet and toast them until they are golden, 7 to 10 minutes. Let them cool completely. Scatter the toasted nuts over the pie before serving.

3 tablespoons cold water

1 envelope unflavored gelatin

1 cup full-fat sour cream

½ cup honey

1½ cups heavy cream, chilled

1 prepared crumb crust

½ cup sliced almonds

CHOOSING A CRUST

Plain **Graham Cracker Crust** (page 11) or **Zwieback Crust** (page 16) is best here.

DRESSING IT UP

I usually serve this pie plain, the better to enjoy its subtle honey flavor.

Strawberry Cheesecake Pie

Makes one 9-inch pie; 6 to 8 servings

Strawberries puréed with cream cheese and a little heavy cream give this pie a beautiful pink color and a powerful berry flavor.

2 tablespoons cold water

2 teaspoons unflavored gelatin

One 8-ounce package cream cheese, softened

¾ cup heavy cream

1 pint fresh strawberries, hulled

⅔ cup sugar

1 teaspoon pure vanilla extract

1 prepared crumb crust

1. Place the cold water in a small bowl and sprinkle the gelatin on top. Let the gelatin stand to dissolve. In the workbowl of a food processor, combine the cream cheese, heavy cream, strawberries, sugar, and vanilla and process the mixture until it is smooth.

2. Put 1 inch of water in a small saucepan and bring the pot to a bare simmer. Place the bowl containing the gelatin on top of the simmering water and heat, whisking constantly, just until the gelatin melts, 30 seconds to 1 minute. With the food processor running, pour the gelatin mixture through the feed tube into the strawberry mixture and process to create a smooth purée.

3. Scrape the filling into the prepared pie shell. Cover the pie with plastic wrap and refrigerate it until the filling is completely set, at least 6 hours and up to 1 day.

CHOOSING A CRUST

Graham Cracker and Oatmeal Crumb Crust (page 13), **Vanilla Wafer Crust** (page 17), **Lemon Nut Cookie Crust** (page 19), **Chocolate Cookie Crust** (page 13), and **Oreo Cookie Crust** (page 14) all work well with this versatile filling.

DRESSING IT UP

If you are a fruit person, go with **Graham Cracker** and **Oatmeal Crust**, **Vanilla Wafer Crust**, or **Lemon Nut Cookie Crust** and **Blueberry** or **Blackberry Mash** (page 130) for color contrast. If you favor chocolate, pour the filling into a chocolate crust and serve the pie with **Warm Chocolate Sauce** (page 126) or **Hot Fudge Sauce** (page 127).

Apricot-Almond Mousse Pie

Makes one 9-inch pie; 6 to 8 servings

3 tablespoons cold water

1 envelope unflavored gelatin

1 cup best-quality apricot preserves

¼ cup almond paste, crumbled

1½ cups plain lowfat yogurt

1 cup heavy cream, chilled

1 prepared crumb crust

½ cup sliced almonds

1. Place the cold water in a small bowl and sprinkle the gelatin on top. Let the gelatin stand to dissolve. In the workbowl of a food processor, combine the apricot preserves, almond paste, and yogurt and process the mixture until it is smooth.

2. Put 1 inch of water in a small saucepan and bring the pot to a bare simmer. Place the bowl containing the gelatin on top of the simmering water and heat, whisking constantly, just until the gelatin melts, 30 seconds to 1 minute. Whisk the gelatin mixture into the apricot mixture until the consistency is smooth.

3. In a large mixing bowl using an electric mixer, whip the cream until it holds soft peaks. Gently fold the apricot mixture into the whipped cream.

4. Scrape the filling into the prepared pie shell. Cover the pie with plastic wrap and refrigerate it until the filling is completely set, at least 6 hours and up to 1 day.

5. When you are ready to serve the pie, preheat the oven to 350 degrees. Place the sliced almonds on a baking sheet and toast them until they are golden, 7 to 10 minutes. Let them cool completely. Scatter the toasted nuts over the pie before serving.

Apricot preserves give this pie great fruit flavor without any time-consuming preparation. Tart yogurt balances the sweetness of the preserves and almond paste.

CHOOSING A CRUST
Amaretti Crust (page 18) is the perfect choice. **Lemon Nut Cookie Crust** (page 19) also works well.

DRESSING IT UP
The toasted almonds are enough of a garnish. I pass on other accompaniments.

Cantaloupe and Berry Pie

Makes one 9-inch pie; 6 to 8 servings

This pie is like my favorite smoothie transformed into a dessert. Raspberries and blueberries both go well with cantaloupe, so choose according to either taste or availability.

1. Place the cold water in a small bowl and sprinkle the gelatin on top. Let the gelatin stand to dissolve. In the workbowl of a food processor combine the melon and sugar and process them until the mixture is smooth. Add the yogurt and heavy cream and pulse once or twice to combine.

2. Put 1 inch of water in a small saucepan and bring the pot to a bare simmer. Place the bowl containing the gelatin on top of the simmering water and heat, whisking constantly, just until the gelatin melts, 30 seconds to 1 minute. With the food processor running, scrape the gelatin mixture through the feed tube into the melon mixture and process to combine.

3. Scrape the filling into the prepared pie shell. Scatter the berries evenly over the melon mixture. Cover the pie with plastic wrap and refrigerate it until the filling is completely set, at least 6 hours and up to 1 day.

3 tablespoons cold water

1 envelope unflavored gelatin

½ small ripe cantaloupe, seeded and flesh cut into 1-inch pieces

½ cup sugar

¾ plain lowfat yogurt

¾ cup heavy cream

1 prepared crumb crust

1 cup fresh raspberries or blueberries, picked over for stems

CHOOSING A CRUST

Vanilla Wafer Crust (page 17) is best here; **Zwieback Crust** (page 16) is also good.

DRESSING IT UP

I wouldn't add anything to slices of this pie except maybe a spoonful of whipped cream for richness.

Papaya Mousse Pie

Makes one 9-inch pie; 6 to 8 servings

Frozen tropical fruit chunks and purées are a wonderful resource for the icebox pie maker. Look for the Goya brand in the freezer section of your supermarket. Be sure to drain the papaya well before puréeing it; otherwise your pie will be too watery to set up properly.

2 tablespoons cold water

1 envelope unflavored gelatin

One 14-ounce bag frozen papaya chunks, thawed

3 large eggs

½ cup sugar

¼ teaspoon ground mace or nutmeg

1 cup heavy cream, chilled

1 prepared crumb crust

1. Place the cold water in a small stainless-steel bowl and sprinkle the gelatin over the water. Let the gelatin stand to dissolve.

2. Place the papaya chunks in a strainer and allow the excess liquid to drain. Place the drained papaya chunks in the workbowl of a food processor and process them until they are smooth.

3. Put 2 inches of water in a medium-size saucepan and bring the pot to a bare simmer. Whisk the eggs and sugar together in a medium-size stainless-steel bowl and place the bowl on top of the simmering water, making sure that the bottom of the bowl doesn't touch the water. Heat the egg mixture, whisking constantly, until it registers 160 degrees on an instant-read thermometer.

4. Remove the bowl from the pan and whisk in the gelatin mixture. With an electric mixer beat the egg-and-gelatin mixture until it is cool and thick, about 5 minutes. Beat in the puréed papaya and mace.

5. In another medium-size mixing bowl using an electric mixer, whip the heavy cream until soft peaks form. Gently fold the whipped cream into the papaya mixture.

6. Scrape the filling into the prepared pie shell. Cover the pie with plastic wrap and refrigerate it until the filling is completely set, at least 6 hours and up to 1 day.

CHOOSING A CRUST

Gingersnap Crust (page 16) is wonderful here. For a milder pie, try **Lemon Nut Cookie Crust** (page 19) or **Graham Cracker Crust** (page 11).

DRESSING IT UP

A little whipped cream and chopped **Nougatine** (page 132) on top of each slice are terrific. **Caramel Sauce** (page 129) made with rum adds to the tropical flavor.

Lime-Coconut Pie

Makes one 9-inch pie; 6 to 8 servings

1. Place the cold water in a small stainless-steel bowl and sprinkle the gelatin over the water. Let the gelatin stand until it softens, about 10 minutes.

2. Whisk together the cream of coconut, yogurt, lime juice, and lime zest in a large mixing bowl.

3. Set the bowl of gelatin over a small saucepan of barely simmering water and whisk the gelatin until it dissolves, 30 seconds to 1 minute. Stir the gelatin mixture into the coconut mixture.

4. Pour the filling into the prepared pie shell. Cover the pie with plastic wrap and refrigerate it until the filling is completely set, at least 6 hours and up to 1 day.

This recipe, a version of which appears in Mom's Big Book of Baking, *is easier to make than Key lime pie and has a more pronounced flavor because of the cream of coconut.*

2 tablespoons cold water

2 teaspoons unflavored gelatin

One 15-ounce can cream of coconut, such as Coco Lopez

⅔ cup plain lowfat yogurt

½ cup fresh lime juice

2 teaspoons grated lime zest

1 prepared crumb crust

CHOOSING A CRUST
Graham Cracker Crust (page 11), **Graham Cracker and Coconut Crust** (page 12), or **Vanilla Wafer Crust** (page 17) will work.

DRESSING IT UP
Whipped cream is the natural choice. Spread it all over the pie before slicing or spoon a dollop on each slice. The pie, or individual slices, may also be garnished with lime twists dipped in granulated sugar.

Frozen Cranberry Mousse Pie

Makes one 9-inch pie; 6 to 8 servings

2½ cups fresh or frozen cranberries, picked over for stems

¾ cup sugar

½ cup water

2 large egg whites

1 cup heavy cream, chilled

1 teaspoon pure vanilla extract

1 prepared crumb crust

1. Combine the cranberries, ¼ cup of the sugar, and the water in a heavy medium-size saucepan and bring the pot to a boil. Cook, stirring a few times, until the mixture is thickened, about 5 minutes. Remove the pan from the heat and let the mixture cool completely.

2. Place the egg whites in a large mixing bowl and using an electric mixer whip them on medium speed until they are foamy. Increase the speed to high and add 2 tablespoons of the remaining sugar in a slow, steady stream. Beat the mixture until it holds stiff peaks. Add the remaining 6 tablespoons sugar, heavy cream, and vanilla and beat again until stiff peaks form. Fold in the cranberry mixture.

3. Scrape the mousse into the prepared pie crust. Cover the pie with plastic wrap and refrigerate it until the filling is completely set, at least 6 hours and up to 1 day.

Even after my husband had taste-tested over fifty pies, he couldn't help himself—he had to keep sneaking pieces of this one from the freezer every night until it was gone.

CHOOSING A CRUST

Graham Cracker Crust (page 11), **Zwieback Crust** (page 16), or **Graham Cracker and Oatmeal Crumb Crust** (page 13) would work well here. If you love chocolate, go with **Chocolate Cookie Crust** (page 13).

DRESSING IT UP

Maple Walnut Sauce (page 130) is divine with this pie. For extra cranberry flavor, try **Cranberry Dessert Sauce** (page 131). If you've chosen a chocolate crust, drizzle slices of pie with **Warm Chocolate Sauce** (page 126).

Frozen Prune Mousse Pie

Makes one 9-inch pie; 6 to 8 servings

3½ ounces pitted prunes (about 10 small)

2 tablespoons Armagnac or brandy

¼ teaspoon ground cinnamon

2 large egg whites

¾ cup sugar

1½ cups heavy cream, chilled

1 teaspoon pure vanilla extract

1 prepared crumb crust

CHOOSING A CRUST
Prunes and chocolate are a perfect match, so go with **Chocolate Cookie Crust** (page 13) or **Oreo Cookie Crust** (page 14).

DRESSING IT UP
Garnish each piece of pie with whipped cream and/or **Warm Chocolate Sauce** (page 126) flavored with Armagnac or brandy if you like.

1. Place the prunes in a heat-proof bowl and cover them with boiling water. Let the prunes stand for 10 minutes and then drain them.

2. In the workbowl of a food processor, combine the rehydrated prunes, Armagnac, and cinnamon and process the mixture until it is smooth. Let the mixture cool completely.

3. Place the egg whites in a large mixing bowl and using an electric mixer whip them on medium speed until they are foamy. Increase the speed to high and add 2 tablespoons of the sugar in a slow, steady stream. Beat the mixture until it holds stiff peaks. Add the remaining sugar, the heavy cream, and vanilla and beat the mixture until stiff peaks form. Fold in the prune mixture.

4. Scrape the filling into the prepared pie crust. Cover the pie with plastic wrap and refrigerate it until the filling is completely set, at least 6 hours and up to 1 day.

I've always loved the prune and Armagnac ice cream that is so popular with French pastry chefs. Here's a simple way that I satisfy my craving without actually making my own ice cream. Dressed up, this frozen pie is a sophisticated dinner party dessert. If egg safety is a concern, substitute powdered egg whites for fresh ones.

Toasted Almond Semifreddo Pie

Makes one 9-inch pie; 6 to 8 servings

1. Preheat the oven to 350 degrees. Place the almonds on a baking sheet and bake them until they are golden and fragrant, 5 to 8 minutes. Remove the pan from the oven and let the almonds cool completely.

2. Place the egg whites in a large mixing bowl and using an electric mixer whip them on medium speed until they are foamy. Increase the speed to high and add 2 tablespoons of the sugar in a slow, steady stream. Beat the mixture until it holds stiff peaks. Add the remaining sugar, the heavy cream, espresso powder, and vanilla and beat the mixture until stiff peaks form. Stir in the almonds.

This yummy frozen pie reminds me of that old-style Italian dessert, tortoni. If egg safety is a concern, use powdered egg whites instead of fresh ones.

3. Scrape the filling into the prepared pie crust. Cover the pie with plastic wrap and refrigerate it until the filling is completely set, at least 6 hours and up to 1 day.

¾ cup slivered almonds

2 large egg whites

¾ cup sugar

1½ cups heavy cream, chilled

1½ tablespoons instant espresso powder

1½ teaspoons pure vanilla extract

1 prepared crumb crust

CHOOSING A CRUST
Only **Amaretti Crust** (page 18) will do.

DRESSING IT UP
Drizzle **Warm Chocolate Sauce** (page 126) flavored with almond liqueur over slices of pie.

Chocolate Dream Pies

Light Chocolate Mousse Pie

Gianduia Pie

Chocolate Cream Cheese Pie

White Chocolate and Blueberry Pie

Raspberry–Chocolate Chip
    Mousse Pie

White Chocolate and Raspberry Pie

Rocky Road Pie

Chocolate Pudding Pie

Triple Chocolate Mint Pie

Black Bottom Butterscotch Pie

Chocolate and Honey Pudding Pie

White Chocolate–Mint Pudding Pie

Chocolate-Coconut Pie

Rich Chocolate Mousse Pie

Milk Chocolate and Cherry Pie

White Chocolate Ganache and
    Banana Pie

Frozen Milky Way Pie

Chocolate, so rich and thick on its own, adapts particularly well to the icebox concept. Chocolate puddings, custards, and egg-based and whipped-cream-enriched mousses all have more than enough flavor and body that they can be poured into a crumb crust and allowed to chill into a quick pie.

Chocolate is surprisingly versatile. You can combine it with everything from preserved cherries to coconut to mint to make simple icebox pie fillings. Although every recipe in this chapter contains chocolate, each filling has a distinct character and flavor. There is something to please everyone, and a dessert for every occasion. Homey Chocolate Pudding Pie is the perfect follow-up to a simple family supper. Rich Chocolate Mousse Pie, served with Raspberry Coulis, is elegant enough for entertaining. Frozen desserts such as Rocky Road Pie or White Chocolate and Blueberry Pie can be made a week in advance and served to friends and family on those days when it's just too hot to bake but only pie will do.

There are several ways to turn chocolate into pie filling. Combining melted and cooled chocolate with whipped cream is one of the simplest. For the smoothest, creamiest, lightest fillings, just follow a couple of simple directions. Melt chocolate with care over barely simmering water. (If melted over direct heat, chocolate may separate, losing its sheen, and become grainy.) Don't overwhip the cream or it, too, will lose its smooth texture. Fold the chocolate into the cream thoroughly but gently. Overmixing will deflate the mixture and result in a heavier pie filling. Icebox desserts don't get any simpler or better than Light Chocolate Mousse Pie, an airy but intense chocolate mousse contrasting with the crunch of a crumb crust.

The addition of unflavored gelatin to whipped cream and chocolate makes for

a slightly less ethereal but more stable filling that won't weep or deflate if the weather's hot; the gelatin helps keep the pie ice-free when it is frozen. I like the silky texture that gelatin lends to pie fillings. I add just enough gelatin to give the pie a pleasant firmness, but not so much that the filling has the rubbery consistency of Jell-O. Gelatin is not difficult to work with. Before it is stirred into a filling, it must be dissolved in two steps. First, the granules must be softened in cool water. Then the softened granules must be heated until they melt into a clear liquid. When stirring the melted gelatin into a cool liquid, be sure to whisk it very vigorously so that no rubbery strands form before it is evenly incorporated.

Cornstarch-thickened pudding makes another simple chocolate pie filling. Milk, sugar, and cornstarch are heated in a pan on top of the stove until the mixture is thick and smooth. Then chopped chocolate is stirred in until it is melted. Variations like Black Bottom Butterscotch Pie and Chocolate and Honey Pudding Pie are easy to make once you've mastered the basic technique for making smooth and creamy chocolate pudding. First, make sure to dissolve the cornstarch in a little bit of liquid before stirring it into the rest of the liquid in the pan. Second, whisk the liquid constantly as you heat it, making sure that none of the pudding sticks to the bottom of the pan, where it can form lumps. Third, remove the pan from the heat as soon as the pudding thickens. Overcooking pudding may result in curdling. Pour the hot pudding directly into the pie shell and immediately place plastic wrap directly on the surface of the filling to prevent "pudding skin" from forming.

Chocolate may also be simply thickened with beaten egg yolks and lightened with whipped egg whites, as in Rich Chocolate Mousse Pie. If egg safety is an issue for you but you love the richness of an egg-based chocolate dessert, try a recipe like Milk Chocolate and Cherry Pie, where the eggs are slowly heated over simmering water to a safe temperature of 160 degrees before being incorporated into the filling.

If you like your chocolate straight-up, check out the final two recipes, White Chocolate Ganache and Banana Pie and Frozen Milky Way Pie. In each of these recipes, chocolate is transformed into pie filling in the simplest way possible: After the chocolate is finely chopped, hot cream is poured over it and the mixture is whisked until it is smooth. As the mixture cools in the pie shell, it becomes a dense filling with a truffle-like consistency. There's no easier way to fill a pie shell and, for the true chocoholic, none more satisfying.

A word about buying chocolate: Save the cheap stuff for baking, where the alchemy of the oven transforms mediocre squares sold in the baking aisle into fudgy brownies. For the best-tasting chocolate icebox pies, buy chocolate that you'd enjoy eating out of hand. Premium European brands such as Vahlrona, Callebaut, and Lindt, and the American-made Ghirardelli will give your desserts deep, rich chocolate flavor. It is especially important to be brand-conscious when buying white chocolate, since lower-priced bars contain less cocoa butter, or none at all, and will yield bland fillings with very little chocolate flavor.

Light Chocolate Mousse Pie

Makes one 9-inch pie; 6 to 8 servings

This mousse is made with whipped cream rather than with eggs, in an effort to cut the richness of the chocolate.

1. Put 2 inches of water in a medium-size saucepan and bring the pot to a bare simmer. Combine the chocolate and 2 tablespoons of the heavy cream in a stainless-steel bowl big enough to rest on top of the saucepan. Place the bowl over the simmering water, making sure that the bottom of the bowl doesn't touch the water. Heat, whisking occasionally, until the chocolate is completely melted. Remove the bowl from the heat, stir in the framboise or water, and set the chocolate mixture aside to cool for 5 minutes.

2. In a medium-size mixing bowl using an electric mixer, whip the remaining 1 cup heavy cream and the sugar together until the cream holds stiff peaks. Gently fold the whipped cream into the chocolate mixture.

3. Scrape the mousse into the prepared pie crust, smoothing the surface with a rubber spatula. Cover the pie with plastic wrap and refrigerate it until the filling is completely set, at least 3 hours and up to 1 day.

7 ounces bittersweet chocolate, finely chopped

1 cup plus 2 tablespoons heavy cream, chilled

2 tablespoons framboise or water

2 tablespoons sugar

1 prepared crumb crust

CHOOSING A CRUST
Chocolate Cookie Crust (page 13) or **Chocolate Cookie and Nut Crust** (page 14) underscores the flavor of the mousse.

DRESSING IT UP
Just before serving, use a fine mesh strainer to sift unsweetened cocoa powder over the pie. Spoon some **Raspberry Coulis** (page 131) onto dessert plates and place slices of pie on top.

Gianduia Pie

Makes one 9-inch pie; 6 to 8 servings

¾ cup hazelnuts, toasted and skinned
(see Note)

1½ cups heavy cream, chilled

1 teaspoon pure vanilla extract

One 13-ounce jar Nutella

1 prepared crumb crust

1. Place the skinned hazelnuts in the workbowl of a food processor and chop them very fine.

2. Combine the cream and vanilla in a large mixing bowl and using an electric mixer whip the cream until stiff peaks form.

3. Place the Nutella in a medium-size mixing bowl and stir in one quarter of the whipped cream. Gently fold the lightened Nutella mixture back into the remaining whipped cream. Fold in the chopped hazelnuts.

4. Scrape the filling into the prepared pie shell and smooth the top with a rubber spatula. Cover the pie with plastic wrap and refrigerate it until the filling is completely set, at least 6 hours and up to 1 day.

Note: To toast and skin hazelnuts, place the nuts on a baking sheet and bake them in a preheated 350-degree oven until they are fragrant, about 10 minutes. Remove the pan from the oven, wrap the nuts in a clean kitchen towel, and allow the nuts to cool for 10 to 15 minutes. Rub the nuts with the towel to remove the skins (it's okay if bits of skin stick to some of the nuts).

This pie tastes like Baci, the yummy Italian version of the chocolate kiss. Nutella, a chocolate-and-hazelnut spread, is available in many supermarkets and gourmet stores.

CHOOSING A CRUST
Chocolate Cookie and Nut Crust (page 14) made with skinned hazelnuts would be delicious here. Plain **Chocolate Cookie Crust** (page 13) would do fine, too.

DRESSING IT UP
Chocolate sauce would be overkill. Whipped cream is my choice.

Chocolate Cream Cheese Pie

Makes one 9-inch pie; 6 to 8 servings

12 ounces bittersweet chocolate, finely chopped

1½ cups heavy cream, chilled

¼ cup dark corn syrup

Two 3-ounce packages cream cheese, softened

1 prepared crumb crust

1. Put 2 inches of water in a medium-size saucepan and bring the pot to a bare simmer. Combine the chocolate, ½ cup of the heavy cream, and the corn syrup in a stainless-steel bowl big enough to rest on top of the saucepan. Place the bowl over the simmering water, making sure that the bottom of the bowl doesn't touch the water. Heat, whisking occasionally, until the chocolate is completely melted. Remove the bowl from the heat and set the mixture aside to cool until it is just warm, 5 to 10 minutes. Using an electric mixer, beat in the softened cream cheese until the mixture is smooth.

2. In a medium-size mixing bowl using an electric mixer, whip the remaining 1 cup heavy cream until it just holds stiff peaks. Gently fold the whipped cream into the chocolate mixture.

3. Scrape the filling into the prepared pie crust, smoothing the top with a rubber spatula. Cover the pie with plastic wrap and refrigerate it until the filling is completely set, at least 3 hours and up to 1 day.

For chocolate cheesecake fans, here's a simple no-bake dessert.

CHOOSING A CRUST

Chocolate Cookie Crust (page 13), **Oreo Cookie Crust** (page 14), or **Vanilla Wafer Crust** (page 17) is great here.

DRESSING IT UP

Whipped cream and **Strawberry Mash** (page 130), together or separately, are great on top of this pie. Whipped cream and **Cranberry Dessert Sauce** (page 131) make another terrific combination. Or simply sift some unsweetened cocoa powder over the pie just before serving.

White Chocolate and Blueberry Pie

Makes one 9-inch pie; 6 to 8 servings

This luscious pie makes a wonderful end-of-summer dessert.

1. Place the cold water in a small stainless-steel bowl and sprinkle the gelatin on top. Let the gelatin stand to dissolve.

2. Put 2 inches of water in a medium-size saucepan and bring the pot to a bare simmer. Combine the chocolate, butter, and ½ cup of the heavy cream in a stainless-steel bowl big enough to rest on top of the saucepan. Place the bowl over the simmering water, making sure that the bottom of the bowl doesn't touch the water. Heat, whisking occasionally, until the chocolate is completely melted and the mixture is smooth. Set the mixture aside to cool slightly.

3. In another stainless-steel bowl whisk together the eggs and sugar. Place that bowl over the simmering water, making sure that the bottom of the bowl doesn't touch the water. Heat, whisking constantly, until the egg mixture has thickened and registers 160 degrees on an instant-read thermometer. Remove the bowl from the heat and whisk in the vanilla.

4. Whisk in the white chocolate mixture and the gelatin and continue to stir the mixture off the heat until it is smooth. Set the bowl containing the chocolate-and-egg mixture over a larger bowl of ice cubes and let the mixture stand, whisking occasionally, until it begins to thicken, about 10 minutes.

5. In a medium-size mixing bowl using an electric mixer, whip the remaining 1 cup heavy cream until it holds soft peaks. Gently fold the whipped cream into the chocolate-and-egg mixture. Then fold in the blueberries.

6. Scrape the filling into the prepared pie shell. Cover the pie with plastic wrap and refrigerate it until the filling is completely set, at least 6 hours and up to 1 day.

2 tablespoons cold water

1 teaspoon unflavored gelatin

7 ounces white chocolate, finely chopped

1 tablespoon unsalted butter

1½ cups heavy cream, chilled

2 large eggs

⅓ cup sugar

1 teaspoon pure vanilla extract

2 cups fresh or frozen blueberries, picked over for stems

1 prepared crumb crust

CHOOSING A CRUST
Graham Cracker Crust (page 11), **Vanilla Wafer Crust** (page 17), or **Zwieback Crust** (page 16) will do nicely.

DRESSING IT UP
Warm **Caramel Sauce** (page 129) does the trick here. Or warm up some **Blueberry Mash** (page 130) for a minute or two in the microwave and spoon it over slices of pie.

Raspberry-Chocolate Chip Mousse Pie

Makes one 9-inch pie; 6 to 8 servings

3 tablespoons cold water

1 envelope unflavored gelatin

2 cups fresh or frozen raspberries

½ cup sugar

1½ cups heavy cream, chilled

1 tablespoon framboise or other raspberry-flavored liqueur

1 teaspoon pure vanilla extract

¾ cup miniature semisweet chocolate chips

1 prepared crumb crust

1. Place the cold water in a small stainless-steel bowl and sprinkle the gelatin on top. Let the gelatin stand to dissolve.

2. Combine the raspberries and sugar in a heavy medium-size saucepan over medium-low heat and cook until the sugar has dissolved and the mixture is warm to the touch. Stir in the gelatin mixture. Set the berry mixture aside to cool to room temperature, stirring occasionally, for 10 to 15 minutes.

3. Combine the heavy cream, framboise or other liqueur, and vanilla in a large mixing bowl and using an electric mixer whip the cream until soft peaks form. Gently fold in the raspberry mixture and then the chocolate chips.

4. Scrape the mousse into the prepared pie shell. Cover the pie with plastic wrap and refrigerate it until the filling is completely set, at least 6 hours and up to 1 day.

Since I use a chocolate cookie crust, stir in mini chocolate chips, and top this mousse pie with Warm Chocolate Sauce, I think it's fair to call it a chocolate dessert.

CHOOSING A CRUST
Chocolate Cookie Crust (page 13) or **Oreo Cookie Crust** (page 14) is best here.

DRESSING IT UP
Warm Chocolate Sauce (page 126) made with framboise finishes the pie nicely.

White Chocolate and Raspberry Pie

Makes one 9-inch pie; 6 to 8 servings

2 tablespoons cold water

1 envelope unflavored gelatin

10½ ounces white chocolate

1½ cups heavy cream, chilled

2 tablespoons fresh lemon juice

1 teaspoon grated lemon zest

1 prepared crumb crust

1 pint fresh raspberries

CHOOSING A CRUST
Graham Cracker Crust (page 11) or **Graham Cracker and Nut Crust** (page 11) would be a natural choice. **Lemon Nut Cookie Crust** (page 19) would also work, as would **Vanilla Wafer and Sliced Almond Crust** (page 17).

DRESSING IT UP
Raspberry Coulis (page 131) drizzled on top of and around slices of this pie adds visual and taste appeal.

1. Place the cold water in a small stainless-steel bowl and sprinkle the gelatin on top. Let the gelatin stand to dissolve.

2. Put 2 inches of water in a medium-size saucepan and bring the pot to a bare simmer. Combine the chocolate and ½ cup of the heavy cream in a stainless-steel bowl big enough to rest on top of the saucepan. Place the bowl over the simmering water, making sure that the bottom of the bowl doesn't touch the water. Heat, whisking occasionally, until the chocolate is completely melted and the mixture is smooth.

3. Whisk the gelatin mixture, lemon juice, and lemon zest into the bowl of melted chocolate. Set that bowl over a larger bowl of ice cubes and let it stand, whisking occasionally, until the mixture begins to thicken, about 10 minutes.

4. In a medium-size mixing bowl using an electric mixer, whip the remaining 1 cup heavy cream until soft peaks form. Gently fold the whipped cream into the chocolate mixture.

5. Scrape the filling into the prepared pie shell. Cover the pie with plastic wrap and refrigerate it until the filling is completely set, at least 6 hours and up to 1 day.

6. Just before serving, arrange the raspberries on top of the pie.

This pie tastes like a wonderfully rich, slightly lemony cheesecake, even though it doesn't contain any cream cheese. The white chocolate gives it an unbelievably velvety texture. Strawberries, blueberries, or blackberries may be substituted for the raspberries.

Rocky Road Pie

Makes one 9-inch pie; 6 to 8 servings

2 tablespoons cold water

1 teaspoon unflavored gelatin

3 large egg yolks

6 tablespoons sugar

1 cup brewed espresso or very strong coffee

¼ cup unsweetened cocoa powder

1 cup heavy cream

1 cup miniature marshmallows

½ cup miniature semisweet chocolate chips

½ cup walnuts, coarsely chopped

1 prepared crumb crust

1. Place the cold water in a small stainless-steel bowl and sprinkle the gelatin on top. Let the gelatin stand to dissolve.

2. Combine the egg yolks and sugar in a medium-size mixing bowl and, using an electric mixer, whip the mixture until the yolks are pale yellow and have increased in volume, about 5 minutes.

3. Bring the espresso and cocoa to a boil in a large heavy saucepan, whisking often to dissolve the cocoa. Dribble the espresso mixture a few drops at a time into the egg mixture, whisking constantly. Return the espresso-and-egg mixture to the saucepan and cook over medium-low heat, whisking constantly, until the edges just begin to bubble. Do not overcook or the mixture will curdle.

4. Remove the pot from the heat and whisk in the gelatin. Set the pot aside, whisking occasionally, until the mixture is cool to the touch, about 10 minutes.

5. In a medium-size mixing bowl using an electric mixer, whip the heavy cream until it holds soft peaks. Gently fold the whipped cream into the espresso-and-egg mixture. Fold in the marshmallows, chocolate chips, and nuts.

6. Scrape the filling into the prepared pie shell. Cover the pie with plastic wrap and freeze it until the filling is completely set, at least 6 hours and up to 1 day.

I think of this as an everything-but-the-kitchen-sink kind of pie. For obvious reasons, this one is a kid pleaser.

CHOOSING A CRUST

Graham Cracker Crust (page 11) is good. **Graham Cracker and Chocolate Chip Crust** (page 12) is even better.

DRESSING IT UP

Use whipped cream, **Hot Fudge Sauce** (page 127), **Caramel Sauce** (page 129), **Strawberry Mash** (page 130), or all four at once.

Chocolate Pudding Pie

Makes one 9-inch pie; 6 to 8 servings

Chocolate pudding poured into a pie shell and topped with whipped cream is an icebox classic. It's also simple and foolproof.

6 tablespoons cornstarch

9 tablespoons sugar

3½ cups half-and-half

9 ounces bittersweet chocolate, coarsely chopped

1½ tablespoons unsalted butter

1 teaspoon pure vanilla extract

1 prepared crumb crust

1. Combine the cornstarch and sugar in a heavy medium-size saucepan. Whisk in ½ cup of the half-and-half until the mixture is smooth. Add the remaining half-and-half and bring the pot to a boil, whisking constantly. Continue to cook the mixture over medium-high heat, whisking constantly, until the mixture thickens, 3 to 4 minutes.

2. Remove the pan from the heat and whisk in the chocolate and butter, continuing to whisk until all the chocolate and butter have melted and the pudding is very smooth. Whisk in the vanilla.

3. Scrape the pudding into the prepared pie shell. Place plastic wrap directly on the surface of the filling and refrigerate the pie until the filling is completely set, at least 6 hours and up to 1 day.

CHOOSING A CRUST

I like **Chocolate Cookie Crust** (page 13) because it adds another layer of chocolate flavor. Use **Graham Cracker Crust** (page 11), **Vanilla Wafer Crust** (page 17), or **Zwieback Crust** (page 16) if you want an old-fashioned, down-home dessert.

DRESSING IT UP

Whipped cream, no question. Either cover the whole pie with a layer of whipped cream before slicing, or slice the pie and top each slice with a generous dollop. For a more grown-up treat, substitute **Coffee Whipped Cream** (page 125) for plain. If you really want to go crazy, top either kind of whipped cream with chocolate shavings.

Triple Chocolate Mint Pie

Makes one 9-inch pie; 6 to 8 servings

1. Combine the cornstarch, sugar, and cocoa powder in a heavy medium-size saucepan. Whisk in 1 cup of the half-and-half until the mixture is smooth. Add the remaining half-and-half and bring the pot to a boil, whisking constantly. Continue to cook the mixture over medium-high heat, whisking, until the mixture thickens, 3 to 4 minutes.

2. Remove the pan from the heat and whisk in both types of chocolate and the butter, continuing to whisk until all the chocolate and butter have melted and the pudding is very smooth. Stir in the peppermint extract.

3. Scrape the pudding into the prepared pie shell. Place plastic wrap directly on the surface of the filling and refrigerate the pie until the filling is completely set, at least 6 hours and up to 1 day.

This pie has an unbelievably rich flavor and silky texture. It's one of my all-time favorites and a must for chocolate fanatics.

6 tablespoons cornstarch

1 cup sugar

½ cup unsweetened cocoa powder

3½ cups half-and-half

3½ ounces bittersweet chocolate, coarsely chopped

3 ounces unsweetened chocolate, coarsely chopped

1½ tablespoons unsalted butter

½ teaspoon pure peppermint extract

1 prepared crumb crust

CHOOSING A CRUST

If you like extreme chocolate desserts, use **Chocolate Cookie Crust** (page 13) or **Oreo Cookie Crust** (page 14). If your tastes are more moderate, go with **Graham Cracker Crust** (page 11).

DRESSING IT UP

Give each slice of pie a dollop of whipped cream and garnish it with a mint sprig or an Andes chocolate mint candy or small peppermint patty.

Black Bottom Butterscotch Pie

Makes one 9-inch pie, 6 to 8 servings

Butterscotch pudding poured on top of chocolate pudding makes for the ultimate pudding lover's pie.

For the chocolate pudding:

3 tablespoons cornstarch

¼ cup granulated sugar

1¼ cups half-and-half

4½ ounces bittersweet chocolate, coarsely chopped

1 tablespoon unsalted butter

½ teaspoon pure vanilla extract

For the butterscotch pudding:

3 tablespoons unsalted butter

½ cup firmly packed dark brown sugar

Pinch of salt

3 tablespoons cornstarch

2 cups half-and-half

1 prepared crumb crust

CHOOSING A CRUST

Go with **Graham Cracker Crust** (page 11), **Zwieback Crust** (page 16), or **Chocolate Cookie Crust** (page 13).

DRESSING IT UP

Whipped cream is welcome, with or without a sprinkling of finely chopped **Nougatine** (page 132) for crunch.

1. *To make the chocolate pudding:* Combine the cornstarch and granulated sugar in a heavy medium-size saucepan. Whisk in ½ cup of the half-and-half until the mixture is smooth. Add the remaining ¾ cup half-and-half and bring the pot to a boil, whisking constantly. Continue to cook the mixture over medium-high heat, whisking, until the mixture thickens, 3 to 4 minutes.

2. Remove the pan from the heat and whisk in the chocolate and butter, continuing to whisk until all the chocolate and butter have melted and the pudding is very smooth. Stir in the vanilla. Scrape the pudding into the prepared pie shell and smooth the top with a rubber spatula.

3. *To make the butterscotch pudding:* Combine the butter, brown sugar, and salt in a clean medium-size saucepan. Cook the mixture over low heat, whisking, until the butter is melted and the sugar is dissolved.

4. Combine the cornstarch and ½ cup of the half-and-half in a small mixing bowl and whisk to dissolve. Set the mixture aside.

5. Add the remaining 1½ cups half-and-half to the saucepan and whisk until it is combined with the brown sugar mixture. Add the half-and-half-and-cornstarch mixture to the saucepan, stir to combine, and turn the heat to medium-high. Cook, whisking, until the mixture thickens, 3 to 4 minutes.

6. Scrape the butterscotch pudding into the pie shell and smooth the top layer of pudding with a rubber spatula so that it evenly covers the chocolate pudding. Place plastic wrap directly on the surface of the filling and refrigerate the pie until the filling is completely set, at least 6 hours and up to 1 day.

Chocolate and Honey Pudding Pie

Makes one 9-inch pie; 6 to 8 servings

6 tablespoons cornstarch

3 large eggs

3 cups half-and-half

7 ounces bittersweet chocolate,
  coarsely chopped

½ cup honey

2 tablespoons unsalted butter

¼ teaspoon salt

1 teaspoon pure vanilla extract

1 prepared crumb crust

1. Whisk together the cornstarch, eggs, and ½ cup of the half-and-half in a heavy medium-size saucepan until smooth. Add the remaining 2½ cups half-and-half and bring the pot to a boil, whisking constantly. Continue to cook the mixture over medium-high heat, whisking, until it thickens, 3 to 4 minutes.

2. Remove the pan from the heat and whisk in the chocolate, honey, butter, salt, and vanilla, continuing to whisk until all the chocolate and butter have melted and the pudding is very smooth.

3. Scrape the pudding into the prepared pie shell. Place plastic wrap directly on the surface of the filling and refrigerate the pie until the filling is completely set, at least 6 hours and up to 1 day.

Honey gives this pudding pie an intriguing layer of flavor.

CHOOSING A CRUST
Zwieback Crust (page 16) or **Graham Cracker Crust** (page 11) matches well with chocolate and honey.

DRESSING IT UP
Honey Whipped Cream (page 125) is great here.

White Chocolate–Mint Pudding Pie

Makes one 9-inch pie; 6 to 8 servings

1. Combine the cornstarch and sugar in a heavy medium-size saucepan. Whisk in ½ cup of the half-and-half until the mixture is smooth. Add the remaining 2½ cups half-and-half and the mint and bring the pot to a boil, whisking constantly. Continue to cook the mixture over medium-high heat, whisking, until the mixture thickens, 3 to 4 minutes.

2. Remove the pan from the heat and whisk in the white chocolate, butter, and vanilla, continuing to whisk until all the chocolate and butter have melted and the pudding is very smooth.

3. Pour the pudding through a fine mesh strainer and into the prepared pie shell. Place plastic wrap directly on the surface of the filling and refrigerate the pie until the filling is completely set, at least 6 hours and up to 1 day.

The hint of mint in this pudding pie offsets the sometimes cloying sweetness of white chocolate.

6 tablespoons cornstarch

1 cup sugar

3 cups half-and-half

⅓ cup fresh mint leaves, minced

8 ounces white chocolate, finely chopped

2 tablespoons unsalted butter

1 teaspoon pure vanilla extract

1 prepared crumb crust

CHOOSING A CRUST
I like the way dark chocolate crusts look against the white filling, so I use **Chocolate Cookie Crust** (page 13) or **Oreo Cookie Crust** (page 14) with this one. **Graham Cracker Crust** (page 11) works well also.

DRESSING IT UP
Use **Warm Chocolate Sauce** (page 126) if you like the combination of dark and white chocolate.

Chocolate-Coconut Pie

Makes one 9-inch pie; 6 to 8 servings

6 tablespoons cornstarch

½ cup plus 1 tablespoon sugar

1¾ cups half-and-half

One 14-ounce can unsweetened
coconut milk

9 ounces bittersweet chocolate,
coarsely chopped

1½ tablespoons unsalted butter

1 teaspoon pure coconut extract

1 teaspoon pure vanilla extract

1 prepared crumb crust

¾ cup sweetened flaked coconut

1. Combine the cornstarch and sugar in a heavy medium-size saucepan. Whisk in ½ cup of the half-and-half until the mixture is smooth. Add the remaining 1¼ cups half-and-half and the coconut milk and bring the pot to a boil, whisking constantly. Continue to cook the mixture over medium-high heat, whisking, until the mixture thickens, 3 to 4 minutes.

2. Remove the pan from the heat and whisk in the chocolate, butter, coconut extract, and vanilla extract, continuing to whisk until all the chocolate and butter have melted and the pudding is very smooth.

3. Scrape the pudding into the prepared pie shell. Place plastic wrap directly on the surface of the filling and refrigerate the pie until the filling is completely set, at least 6 hours and up to 1 day.

4. When you are ready to serve the pie, preheat the oven to 350 degrees. Spread the flaked coconut on a baking sheet and toast it until it is golden, stirring once or twice, 5 to 8 minutes. Watch the coconut carefully; it will go from golden to burnt in an instant. Let it cool completely.

5. Just before serving, press the toasted coconut onto the surface of the pie.

Coconut extract, available right near the vanilla in the spice section of the supermarket, really boosts the flavor of this pie.

CHOOSING A CRUST
Graham Cracker and Coconut Crust (page 12), definitely.

DRESSING IT UP
Spoon some **Mango Coulis** (page 131) around each slice of pie for an extra-tropical dessert.

Rich Chocolate Mousse Pie

Makes one 9-inch pie; 6 to 8 servings

Classic chocolate mousse enriched with egg yolks and lightened with whipped egg whites makes a simple and wonderful pie filling.

8 ounces bittersweet chocolate, finely chopped

6 tablespoons (¾ stick) unsalted butter

3 tablespoons orange- or coffee-flavored liqueur

5 large eggs, separated

½ cup sugar

1 prepared crumb crust

1. Put 2 inches of water in a medium-size saucepan and bring the pot to a bare simmer. Combine the chocolate and butter in a stainless-steel bowl big enough to rest on top of the saucepan. Place the bowl over the simmering water, making sure that the bottom of the bowl doesn't touch the water. Heat, whisking occasionally, until the chocolate and butter are completely melted. Remove the bowl from the heat, whisk in the liqueur, and set the mixture aside.

2. Place the egg yolks and sugar in a large mixing bowl and using an electric mixer beat the egg yolks on high speed until they are thick and pale, about 5 minutes. Beat in the chocolate mixture. Wash and thoroughly dry the beaters.

3. In a large mixing bowl using an electric mixer, beat the egg whites with the clean beaters until they just hold stiff peaks. Stir about one-third of the whites into the chocolate-and-egg-yolk mixture to lighten it. Gently fold in the remaining egg whites until no white streaks remain.

4. Scrape the mousse into the prepared pie shell. Cover the pie with plastic wrap and refrigerate it until the filling is completely set, at least 6 hours and up to 1 day.

CHOOSING A CRUST
Chocolate Cookie Crust (page 13) or **Chocolate Cookie and Nut Crust** (page 14) makes for the most sophisticated dessert.

DRESSING IT UP
There are two ways to go here. Use coffee liqueur in the pie and top each slice with a dollop of **Coffee Whipped Cream** (page 125), or use orange liqueur in the pie and serve each slice with **Cranberry Dessert Sauce** (page 131) for a really unusual and festive dessert that would be great to serve for the holidays.

Note: Raw eggs should not be used in food to be consumed by children, pregnant women, elderly people, or anyone in poor health or with a compromised immune system. Make sure you use the freshest eggs possible.

Milk Chocolate and Cherry Pie

Makes one 9-inch pie; 6 to 8 servings

Preserved cherries (canned sour or sweet cherries, not canned cherry filling) are a wonderful convenience. Just make sure to pat them dry so that your filling won't be too watery.

1. Arrange the cherries on the bottom of the pie crust.

2. Put 2 inches of water in a medium-size saucepan and bring the pot to a bare simmer. Combine the chocolate, sugar, and heavy cream in a stainless-steel bowl big enough to rest on top of the saucepan. Place the bowl over the simmering water, making sure that the bottom of the bowl doesn't touch the water. Heat, whisking occasionally, until the chocolate is completely melted.

3. Whisk in the eggs one at a time. Heat, whisking constantly, until the mixture has thickened and registers 160 degrees on an instant-read thermometer.

4. Scrape the mixture over the cherries. Let the filling cool to room temperature. Cover the pie with plastic wrap and refrigerate it until the filling is completely set, at least 6 hours and up to 1 day.

1 cup preserved cherries, drained, patted dry, and halved

1 prepared crumb crust

7½ ounces best-quality milk chocolate

6 tablespoons sugar

1½ cups cup heavy cream

3 large eggs

CHOOSING A CRUST
Go with **Chocolate Cookie Crust** (page 13), **Graham Cracker Crust** (page 11), or **Zwieback Crust** (page 16).

DRESSING IT UP
Whipped cream is all that's needed.

White Chocolate Ganache and Banana Pie

Makes one 9-inch pie; 6 to 8 servings

2 small ripe bananas, peeled and cut into ¼-inch-thick rounds

1 prepared crumb crust

10½ ounces white chocolate

3 tablespoons unsalted butter

1 cup heavy cream

1. Arrange the bananas in the bottom of the prepared pie shell.

2. Put 2 inches of water in a medium-size saucepan and bring the pot to a bare simmer. Combine the white chocolate, butter, and ½ cup of the heavy cream in a stainless-steel bowl big enough to rest on top of the saucepan. Place the bowl over the simmering water, making sure that the bottom of the bowl doesn't touch the water. Heat, whisking occasionally, until the chocolate and butter are completely melted and the mixture is smooth. Transfer the contents to a medium-size mixing bowl and set aside to cool to room temperature.

3. Add the remaining ½ cup heavy cream to the chocolate mixture and using an electric mixer beat the mixture until it holds soft peaks. Scrape the filling over the bananas in the pie shell, smoothing the top with a rubber spatula. Cover the pie with plastic wrap and refrigerate it until the filling is completely set, at least 6 hours and up to 1 day.

This pie satisfies my craving for the combination of white chocolate and bananas. As a plus, it's probably one of the simplest pies in the book.

CHOOSING A CRUST
Graham Cracker Crust (page 11) or **Graham Cracker and Nut Crust** (page 11) is best here.

DRESSING IT UP
Stir ½ cup chopped pecans into some warm **Caramel Sauce** (page 129) flavored with rum and spoon the sauce over slices of pie.

Frozen Milky Way Pie

Makes one 9-inch pie; 6 to 8 servings

1. Combine the chocolate and cocoa in a large mixing bowl.

2. Bring the heavy cream just to a boil in a small saucepan over medium-low heat. Pour the hot cream over the chocolate and cocoa and let the mixture stand for 5 minutes. Whisk it until it is smooth. Pour the chocolate mixture through a fine mesh strainer into the prepared pie shell. Let the filling stand for 15 minutes to cool.

3. Stir the nuts into the caramel sauce. Drop the caramel-and-nut mixture by heaping tablespoonfuls across the top of the pie and swirl the filling with a knife to create a marbling effect. Cover the pie with plastic wrap and freeze it until the filling is completely set, at least 6 hours and up to 1 day.

I love to eat little Milky Way candy bars straight from the freezer. They inspired me to create this filling, which is just milk chocolate ganache swirled with caramel sauce.

12½ ounces best-quality milk chocolate, finely chopped

2 tablespoons unsweetened cocoa powder

1¼ cups heavy cream

1 prepared crumb crust

½ cup walnuts or pecans, coarsely chopped

1 recipe Caramel Sauce (page 129), cooled to room temperature

CHOOSING A CRUST
I like plain **Graham Cracker Crust** (page 11) best with this very sweet filling.

DRESSING IT UP
Top each slice with a small scoop of vanilla or coffee ice cream.

Fruit and Cream Combos

Caramelized Pineapple and Cream Cheese Pie

Kiwi and Cream Pie

Cherry and Mascarpone Cream Pie

Ricotta Cream Pie with Blood Oranges

Raspberry and Cocoa Mascarpone Cream Pie

Custard and Pear Pie

Rhubarb and Rice Pudding Pie

Lime Cream and Strawberry Pie

White Chocolate Tapioca Pie with Mangoes

Couscous and Apricot Pudding Pie

What do you get when you combine a crisp crumb crust, creamy filling, and juicy fruit? Done right, you get a perfect pie, each part contributing delicious flavor and texture to the finished product and enhancing the other parts in the process.

The formula is flexible. Whatever kind of creamy fillings and fruity toppings you favor, there's a way to combine them in a pie shell so that they add up perfectly. Starting with a crust, cream, and fruit, I've come up with homey versions such as Custard and Pear Pie and exotic examples such as Couscous and Apricot Pudding Pie. There are even ways to satisfy chocolate lovers. Try White Chocolate Tapioca Pie with Mangoes or Raspberry and Cocoa Mascarpone Cream Pie if you have trouble deciding between fruit and chocolate desserts.

The most basic way to construct a fruit and cream icebox pie is by whipping cream (I like to add a little sour cream to the heavy cream for flavor and body) and topping it with fresh, uncooked fruit. The Kiwi and Cream Pie is an example of this simple construction. Other fruits may be substituted. When choosing fruit to top whipped cream, avoid heavy, very moist fruit, which will deflate the cream. Raspberries or thinly sliced strawberries work well. So do halved seedless grapes. Be sure your fruit is ripe and sweet, since you won't be adding sugar to it. The crust and filling may be made in advance, but don't put a pie like this together until the last moment, or the filling and topping will make the crust soggy.

Cream cheese, its Italian cousin mascarpone, and ricotta cheese make richer, denser cream fillings for icebox pies. On their own, these cheeses are a little too thick. Whipped together with a little heavy cream, they are just light enough to spread into a crumb crust but still

heavy enough to support juicier fruits such as pineapple, cherries, and oranges. These fillings contain less moisture than does plain whipped cream, and they are less delicate. Therefore they can be placed in pie crusts well in advance of serving.

Vanilla custard and lime curd must be cooked and chilled before they can be used in pie filling, so they take a little more time and effort. The result is a more "finished" dessert, for those times when uncooked fillings seem too casual. Both of these cooked cream fillings contain eggs, so in preparing them you should whisk the mixture constantly over low heat until it is thick in order to create perfectly smooth custard. But don't stress out about a few lumps. Pouring the custard through a fine strainer will eliminate the lumps.

Finally, unusual pies can be made with rice, couscous, or tapioca pudding and fruit. These puddings, made with grains or grainy starches, have a little more character than the other fillings do, although they are still soft and creamy enough to qualify as comfort food. If you are looking for fruit and cream with a twist, Rhubarb and Rice Pudding Pie is a delicious way to surprise your guests.

I've suggested ways to dress up fruit and cream pies when appropriate, but one of the nice things about this type of pie is that it usually doesn't need much in the way of accompaniment. The three components—crust, cream, and fruit— form a complete and utterly satisfying package on their own.

Caramelized Pineapple and Cream Cheese Pie

Makes one 9-inch pie; 6 to 8 servings

Sautéing pineapple rings with brown sugar intensifies the flavor of the fruit and makes a quick sauce for the pie. To save time, I buy peeled and cored fresh pineapple that has been vacuum packed.

One 8-ounce package cream cheese, softened

½ cup sour cream

½ cup granulated sugar

½ cup heavy cream, chilled

1 teaspoon pure vanilla extract

1 prepared crumb crust

5 tablespoons unsalted butter

¼ cup firmly packed dark brown sugar

1 ripe pineapple, peeled, cored, and cut into ¼-inch-thick rings

¼ cup dark rum

1. Combine the cream cheese, sour cream, and granulated sugar in a large mixing bowl and using an electric mixer beat the mixture until it is smooth. Wash and dry the beaters.

2. In a medium-size mixing bowl using an electric mixer, whip the heavy cream and vanilla together until soft peaks form. Gently fold the whipped cream into the cream cheese mixture.

3. Scrape the mixture into the prepared pie shell. Cover the pie with plastic wrap and refrigerate it until the filling is completely set, at least 6 hours and up to 1 day.

4. When you are ready to serve the pie, heat the butter and brown sugar together in a large skillet over medium heat until they are melted. Add the pineapple rings and cook them, turning once, until they are golden on each side, 5 to 7 minutes. Transfer the slices to a plate to cool slightly, leaving any juices in the pan.

5. Place individual slices of pie on dessert plates and top with the warm pineapple rings. Bring the juices in the pan to a simmer over medium-high heat. Stir in the rum and cook, stirring frequently, until most of the alcohol has burned off, 2 to 3 minutes. Drizzle some of the warm sauce over each slice of pie and serve immediately.

CHOOSING A CRUST

Graham Cracker and Nut Crust (page 11) adds a nice crunch.

DRESSING IT UP

This pie comes fully dressed, although a little chopped **Nougatine** (page 132) sprinkled over each slice wouldn't hurt.

Kiwi and Cream Pie

Makes one 9-inch pie; 6 to 8 servings

1 cup heavy cream, chilled

¼ cup confectioners' sugar

⅓ cup sour cream

1 prepared crumb crust

4 kiwis, peeled and cut into
⅛-inch-thick rounds

1. Combine the heavy cream and confectioners' sugar in a medium-size mixing bowl and using an electric mixer fitted with the whisk attachment beat the cream until it holds soft peaks. Add the sour cream and beat until the mixture holds soft peaks again. (At this stage the whipped cream may be covered with plastic wrap and refrigerated for up to 6 hours. Re-whisk the cream by hand for a few seconds before using it.)

2. Just before serving, scrape the whipped cream mixture into the prepared crust and smooth the top with a spatula. Arrange the kiwis over the cream, overlapping them to form concentric rings.

This is a lovely, very simple pie that can be made in a flash. Don't assemble it until the last minute, or the moisture from the fruit will begin to water down the cream.

CHOOSING A CRUST
Vanilla Wafer Crust (page 17) adds the right amount of sweetness to this rather tart pie.

DRESSING IT UP
Raspberry Coulis (page 131) or **Mango Coulis** (page 131) adds flavor and color.

Cherry and Mascarpone Cream Pie

Makes one 9-inch pie; 6 to 8 servings

8 ounces mascarpone cheese, softened

½ cup heavy cream, chilled

¼ cup confectioners' sugar

1 teaspoon pure vanilla extract

1 prepared crumb crust

½ cup plus 1 tablespoon water

1 tablespoon cornstarch

⅓ cup granulated sugar

1 pound fresh or frozen sweet cherries, pitted

1 teaspoon fresh lemon juice

2 tablespoons Kirsch

1. Combine the mascarpone, heavy cream, confectioners' sugar, and vanilla in a large mixing bowl and using an electric mixer beat the mixture until it is smooth. Scrape the mixture into the prepared pie shell. Cover the pie with plastic wrap and refrigerate it until it is needed.

2. Combine 1 tablespoon of the water and the cornstarch in a small bowl and stir to dissolve the cornstarch. Combine the remaining ½ cup water and the granulated sugar in a medium-size saucepan and bring the pot to a boil, stirring until the sugar is completely dissolved. Add the cherries, reduce the heat to medium-low, and simmer the cherries until they are softened but have not begun to fall apart, 2 to 3 minutes. Stir in the cornstarch mixture and cook until the juices thicken, another minute. Remove the pan from the heat, stir in the lemon juice and Kirsch, and let the mixture cool completely.

3. Spoon the cooled cherries over the mascarpone-and-cream mixture in the prepared crust. Cover the pie with plastic wrap and refrigerate it until the filling is completely set, at least 3 hours and up to 1 day.

Cherry-covered cheesecake is a dessert cliché, but here's a fresh and interesting variation. A rich and slightly tangy layer of Italian-style cream cheese is covered with a juicy cherry topping.

CHOOSING A CRUST

Use sturdy **Graham Cracker Crust** (page 11) or **Zwieback Crust** (page 16) to hold everything in this pie.

DRESSING IT UP

There is no need for accompaniments, with the cherry topping and creamy mascarpone filling.

Ricotta Cream Pie with Blood Oranges

Makes one 9-inch pie; 6 to 8 servings

1. Combine the ricotta, confectioners' sugar, heavy cream, vanilla, and lemon zest in a medium-size mixing bowl with a wooden spoon. Scrape the mixture into the prepared crust, cover the pie with plastic wrap, and refrigerate it until the filling is completely set, at least 3 hours and up to 1 day.

Removing the tough membranes from each section of orange is rather labor intensive, but the melt-in-your-mouth result is well worth the effort. Blood oranges have a beautiful ruby red color. Regular oranges won't be as pretty, but if you need to substitute them, they will taste just as good.

2. When you are ready to serve the pie, working over a bowl to catch the juices, use a sharp paring knife to remove the membranes from each orange section. Drop the sections into the bowl with the juices. Stir in the granulated sugar and liqueur and let the mixture stand, stirring once or twice, until the sugar is dissolved.

3. To serve, place individual slices of pie on dessert plates and spoon some orange sections and juice over each slice.

1½ pounds whole-milk ricotta cheese (3 cups)

½ cup confectioners' sugar

¼ cup heavy cream, chilled

1 teaspoon pure vanilla extract

½ teaspoon grated lemon zest

1 prepared crumb crust

6 blood oranges or navel oranges, peeled

2 tablespoons granulated sugar

1 tablespoon orange liqueur

CHOOSING A CRUST
Lemon Nut Cookie Crust (page 19) is my favorite here, although **Graham Cracker Crust** (page 11) is good, too.

DRESSING IT UP
Chocolate shavings would taste great and look pretty. Otherwise, I'd skip the accompaniments so the focus stays on the exotic oranges.

Raspberry and Cocoa Mascarpone Cream Pie

Makes one 9-inch pie, 6 to 8 servings

3 tablespoons raspberry jam

1 prepared crumb crust

8 ounces mascarpone cheese

½ cup heavy cream, chilled

¼ cup confectioners' sugar

1 tablespoon unsweetened cocoa powder

1 pint fresh raspberries

1. Spread the jam across the bottom of the prepared crust using a small rubber spatula. Refrigerate the crust while you continue with the recipe.

2. Combine the mascarpone, heavy cream, confectioners' sugar, and cocoa in a large mixing bowl and using an electric mixer beat the mascarpone mixture until it is smooth. Spread the mascarpone mixture over the jam. (At this point, the pie may be refrigerated for up to 1 day before you continue with the recipe.) Cover the pie with plastic wrap and refrigerate it until the filling is completely set.

3. Just before serving, arrange as many raspberries as will fit on top of the cocoa mascarpone. Place slices of pie on individual dessert plates and scatter any remaining raspberries around each slice.

A little bit of unsweetened cocoa powder added to mascarpone makes a wonderful base for fresh raspberries. Any berries that don't fit on top of the filling can be scattered around each slice just before serving.

CHOOSING A CRUST
Definitely **Chocolate Cookie Crust** (page 13) here.

DRESSING IT UP
This pie is terrific plain, but a little **Warm Chocolate Sauce** (page 126) makes it even better. **Raspberry Coulis** (page 131) is another way to go.

Custard and Pear Pie

Makes one 9-inch pie; 6 to 8 servings

This comforting combination of vanilla custard and sautéed pears appeals to kids and adults. The custard and fruit may be made up to a day in advance, but don't put the pears on the pie until just before serving or your filling will become watery.

2 large eggs

¾ cup sugar

¼ cup cornstarch

1½ cups milk

½ cup heavy cream

3 tablespoons unsalted butter

2 teaspoons pure vanilla extract

1 prepared crumb crust

3 ripe pears, peeled, cored, and cut into ¼-inch-thick slices

1. Whisk together the eggs, ½ cup of the sugar, and the cornstarch in a medium-size mixing bowl until smooth.

2. Combine the milk and heavy cream in a medium-size saucepan and bring to a boil. Slowly whisk about ½ cup of the milk-and-cream mixture into the egg mixture. Whisk the egg mixture back into the remaining milk-and-cream mixture in the saucepan and return the pan to the heat. Bring the mixture to a simmer over medium heat, whisking constantly. Cook until the custard has thickened, 1 to 2 minutes. Pour the hot custard through a fine strainer and into a glass bowl. Stir in 1 tablespoon of the butter and the vanilla. Scrape the custard into the prepared crust, place plastic wrap directly on the surface of the filling and refrigerate the pie until the filling is completely set, at least 3 hours and up to 1 day.

3. Heat the remaining 2 tablespoons butter in a large skillet over medium-high heat. When the butter is bubbling, add the pears and the remaining ¼ cup sugar and cook, stirring occasionally, until the pears begin to brown and most of the juices have evaporated, 4 to 5 minutes. Transfer the pears to a platter and let them cool completely. (The cooked pears may be covered with plastic and refrigerated for up to 1 day.)

4. Just before serving, arrange the pears on top of the custard.

CHOOSING A CRUST
Vanilla Wafer Crust (page 17) is just perfect with this combination.

DRESSING IT UP
Whipped cream and **Warm Chocolate Sauce** (page 126) are heavenly with pears and custard.

Rhubarb and Rice Pudding Pie

Makes one 9-inch pie; 6 to 8 servings

1. Combine the rhubarb, sugar, and cinnamon in a large saucepan and bring the pot to a boil over medium-high heat. Reduce the heat and cook the mixture at a bare simmer, stirring occasionally, until the rhubarb has fallen apart and thickened, 15 to 20 minutes. Set the rhubarb aside to cool completely. (The cooled topping may be covered with plastic wrap and refrigerated for up to 3 days.)

2. Combine the rice, milk, sugar, and salt in a large saucepan and bring the pot to a boil. Reduce the heat to medium-low and simmer, uncovered, until the rice is tender and most of the milk is absorbed, 35 to 40 minutes.

3. Bring the heavy cream to a boil in a small saucepan. Whisk the egg in a small mixing bowl to break it up. Very slowly whisk the boiling cream, a bit at a time, into the egg (don't add the cream all at once or the egg will cook and curdle). Stir the egg-and-cream mixture into the pot of rice and simmer, stirring occasionally, until the rice mixture begins to thicken, 3 to 4 minutes. Remove the pan from the heat and stir in the vanilla. Scrape the pudding into the prepared crust. Place plastic wrap directly on the surface of the filling and refrigerate the pie until the filling is completely set, 3 to 4 hours.

4. Spread the cooled rhubarb over the rice pudding, cover the pie with plastic wrap, and refrigerate it until the filling is completely set, another 2 hours or up to 1 day.

Rhubarb cooked down to a jamlike consistency makes a not-too-sweet fruit topping for rich rice pudding.

For the rhubarb topping:
1¼ pounds trimmed fresh or frozen rhubarb stalks, stringed and cut into 1-inch pieces

¾ cup sugar

⅛ teaspoon ground cinnamon

For the rice pudding:
¾ cup long-grain rice

4 cups milk

½ cup plus 2 tablespoons sugar

Pinch of salt

¾ cup heavy cream

1 large egg

½ teaspoon pure vanilla extract

1 prepared crumb crust

CHOOSING A CRUST
Gingersnap Crust (page 16) is wonderful with the rhubarb. **Graham Cracker Crust** (page 11) works as well.

DRESSING IT UP
Serve slices of pie with dollops of whipped cream if you like. **Strawberry Mash** (page 130) is good if you crave the combination of strawberry and rhubarb.

Lime Cream and Strawberry Pie

Makes one 9-inch pie; 6 to 8 servings

4 large eggs

1 cup sugar

1 tablespoon grated lime zest

½ cup fresh lime juice

½ cup (1 stick) unsalted butter, cut into 8 pieces

½ cup heavy cream, chilled

1 prepared crumb crust

2 cups fresh strawberries, hulled and thinly sliced

Lime and strawberries are an unusual pairing, but they seem perfectly natural in this colorful pie.

1. Combine the eggs, sugar, and lime zest in a heavy saucepan and whisk until smooth. Add the lime juice and butter and cook over medium heat, whisking constantly, until the mixture is thickened, 7 to 9 minutes. Do not allow the mixture to come to a boil. Pour the hot lime curd through a fine strainer into a glass bowl. Place plastic wrap directly on the surface of the lime curd. Refrigerate the lime curd until it is cold and thick, at least 3 hours and up to 3 days.

2. In a medium-size mixing bowl using an electric mixer, whip the heavy cream until soft peaks form. Gently fold the whipped cream into the lime curd and then scrape the filling into the prepared pie shell. Cover the pie with plastic wrap and refrigerate it until the filling is completely set, at least 6 hours and up to 1 day.

3. Just before serving, arrange the strawberry slices in concentric circles on top of the filling.

CHOOSING A CRUST
Vanilla Wafer Crust (page 17) is the simplest way to go. **Lemon Nut Cookie Crust** (page 19) or **Amaretti Crust** (page 18) will add an extra layer of flavor.

DRESSING IT UP
There's no need for accompaniments with this pie. Garnish each slice with a sprig of fresh mint if you like.

White Chocolate Tapioca Pie with Mangoes

Makes one 9-inch pie; 6 to 8 servings

¼ cup quick-cooking tapioca

6 tablespoons sugar

¼ teaspoon salt

3 large eggs

3 cups half-and-half

2 ounces white chocolate, finely chopped

1 teaspoon pure vanilla extract

1 prepared crumb crust

2 ripe mangoes, peeled, pitted, and cut into ¼-inch-thick slices

1. Place the tapioca, sugar, salt, eggs, and half-and-half in a medium-size saucepan and whisk to combine. Let the mixture stand for 5 minutes without stirring to allow the tapioca to swell. Cook the tapioca mixture over medium-high heat, stirring, until it comes to a boil. Simmer the pudding for 1 minute and remove the pot from the heat. Stir in the white chocolate and vanilla until the chocolate is melted.

2. Scrape the pudding into a medium-size mixing bowl and place that bowl in a larger bowl of ice cubes. Let the pudding stand, stirring once or twice, until it has thickened but is still warm, 3 to 4 minutes. Scrape the pudding into the prepared crust, place plastic wrap directly on the surface of the filling and refrigerate the pie until the filling is completely set, at least 3 hours and up to 1 day.

3. Just before serving, arrange the mango slices on top of the pie.

White chocolate stirred into tapioca makes for an indescribably delicious pudding. I like tropical fruit on top of tapioca, and mango is my absolute favorite. Choose mangoes that are ripe but still pretty firm. Mangoes that are very soft are difficult to cut into neat, pretty slices.

CHOOSING A CRUST
Graham Cracker and Coconut Crust (page 12) is yummy with this combination, as is plain **Graham Cracker Crust** (page 11).

DRESSING IT UP
This pie is delicious plain, but if you are a real white chocolate fanatic, drizzle **Warm White Chocolate Sauce** (page 126) over each slice.

Couscous and Apricot Pudding Pie

Makes one 9-inch pie; 6 to 8 servings

Couscous plumped with half-and-half and enriched with eggs makes a tasty and unusual pie filling. Other dried fruit and coordinating jams may be substituted for the apricots. Try dried sour cherries with cherry preserves or dried strawberries with strawberry preserves, if you like.

3 cups half-and-half

6 tablespoons sugar

⅛ teaspoon salt

2 large egg yolks, lightly beaten

¾ cup couscous

½ cup dried apricots, finely chopped

⅛ teaspoon ground nutmeg

1 teaspoon pure vanilla extract

1 prepared crumb crust

½ cup apricot preserves

1. Combine the half-and-half, sugar, and salt in a medium-size saucepan and bring the pot to a boil.

2. Slowly dribble about ½ cup of the hot half-and-half mixture into the egg yolks, whisking constantly. Whisk the yolk mixture into the saucepan. Add the couscous, apricots, and nutmeg, and stir to combine. Reduce the heat to medium-low and simmer, whisking constantly, until the mixture thickens and almost all the liquid has been absorbed, 5 to 7 minutes. Remove the pan from the heat and stir in the vanilla.

3. Scrape the hot couscous mixture into the prepared crust and smooth the top with a rubber spatula.

4. Place the apricot preserves in a food processor and process them until they are smooth. Smooth the preserves over the couscous with a spatula. Place plastic wrap directly on the surface of the filling and refrigerate the pie until the filling is completely set, at least 3 hours and up to 1 day, before serving.

CHOOSING A CRUST
Graham Cracker and Nut Crust (page 11) made with pistachios goes perfectly with the Middle Eastern combination of couscous and apricots.

DRESSING IT UP
Sugared Pistachio Nuts (page 132), or just plain chopped pistachios, are nice but not essential.

Ice Cream Parlor Pies

Date and Almond Ice Cream Pie

Chocolate-Almond-Ginger
   Ice Cream Pie

Cookies and Cream Ice Cream Pie

Chocolate-Mint Sorbet Pie

Cranberry and Butterscotch Chip
   Ice Cream Pie

Caramel and Cinnamon
   Ice Cream Pie

Trail Mix Pie

Peanut Butter Cup Pie

Mango and Coconut
   Ice Cream Pie

Raspberry and Lemon Frozen
   Yogurt Pie

Peach Sorbet and Blueberry
   Ice Cream Pie

Pistachio and Orange
   Ice Cream Pie

Strawberry-Almond Heath Bar
   Ice Cream Pie

Coffee Heath Bar Ice Cream Pie

Banana Split Ice Cream Pie

Cherry and Chocolate Chunk
   Ice Cream Pie

S'Mores Pie

Because I was born in July, my mother always served ice cream cake at my birthday party. I used to love the way that an everyday treat like ice cream could be shaped into a "real" dessert for a special occasion.

I feel the same way now about ice cream pie. With a few simple steps, I can transform a couple of pints of Häagen-Dazs into an extraordinary dessert. If I've invited another family over for dinner, I'll make a S'Mores Pie by mixing a couple of chopped up Hershey Bars into the ice cream, pouring it into a Graham Cracker Crust, topping it with a layer of Marshmallow Fluff, and serving it with hot fudge. If I want something a little more grown-up, I'll layer pistachio ice cream and orange sorbet in a prepared pie shell and top slices with Warm White Chocolate Sauce and Sugared Pistachio Nuts.

Ice cream pie is a busy cook's fantasy—a dessert that can be assembled in minutes and frozen for up to a month before serving. But it can also be a passionate cook's dream. A cookie crumb crust functions like a grown-up ice cream cone, holding fun and sophisticated combinations of ice cream and embellishments. Armed with a variety of crumb crust recipes, premium ice cream flavors, and toppings, your possibilities are endless.

All of the recipes in this chapter call for store-bought ice cream. I have nothing against homemade ice cream. In fact, I love it. But because making ice cream is a project in itself and would unnecessarily complicate what should be a simple task, I usually buy a premium brand, which will add richness and flavor to any pie. Expensive ice cream is packaged in pints, two of which will fill a prepared pie shell perfectly. When I'm being economical or watching calories, I'll buy a cheaper ice cream with less butterfat. The crust, mix-ins, and toppings will add plenty of interest to the humblest store brand.

The simplest way to make an ice cream pie is to stir flavoring ingredients into the softened ice cream, then just smooth the mixture into a crust. It's true that you can now buy ice cream with a lot of stuff already mixed in. But doing it yourself allows you to choose your favorite combinations and add as much as you like.

Layering is another way to go. Alternate bands of ice cream with nuts or bits of candy, or layer different flavors of ice cream, frozen yogurt, and sorbet. Rather than serve slices of pie with dollops of whipped cream, you can top a layer of ice cream with a layer of whipped cream and freeze the whole thing. The whipped cream freezes to the consistency of a very light frozen mousse or semifreddo, contrasting nicely with the denser ice cream below. Add some extra sugar to whipped cream that's going to be frozen, since low temperature mutes sweetness.

Ice cream must be softened before it can be smoothed into a pie shell, but it should not be so warm that it has begun to melt. You can let it stand at room temperature to soften for 10 to 20 minutes, depending on how hard the ice cream was to begin with. But the absolute best trick I've found is to soften ice cream in the microwave. Because the microwave heats things from the inside out, it is perfect for softening the rock-hard core of a container of ice cream without melting the warmer outer portion. I own a very powerful microwave that softens my ice cream to the perfect consistency in five seconds flat. It will take you a few tries to figure out how many seconds your particular oven requires. Start with five and work your way up until your ice cream is ready to work with.

Likewise, slicing and serving an ice cream pie is easier when the pie has been allowed to soften on the counter for 10 minutes or has been softened for a few seconds in the microwave. A softer pie also tastes better. If you eat an ice cream pie when it is too cold, your taste buds will be numbed before you can register any pleasure.

Don't neglect the accompaniments when preparing your ice cream pie. You wouldn't serve a sundae without hot fudge and whipped cream; an ice cream pie should also be dressed up to signal that it is a special indulgence.

Date and Almond Ice Cream Pie

Makes one 9-inch pie

½ cup whole almonds

2 pints coffee ice cream, softened

1 cup pitted dates, coarsely chopped

1 prepared crumb crust

1. Preheat the oven to 350 degrees. Place the almonds on a baking sheet and toast them until they are fragrant, 7 to 10 minutes. Remove the pan from the oven and let the almonds cool completely. Coarsely chop the nuts.

2. Combine the ice cream, nuts, and dates in a large mixing bowl and mash the mixture with the back of a wooden spoon until all the ingredients are well combined.

3. Turn the ice cream mixture into the prepared crust and smooth the top with the back of a spoon. Cover the pie with plastic wrap and freeze it until the filling is completely set, at least 3 hours and up to 1 week.

This flavor combination makes for a rather sophisticated dessert. It's terrific at the end of a Mediterranean-inspired meal.

CHOOSING A CRUST
Graham Cracker and Nut Crust (page 11) is delicious here. If you really love almonds, try the **Amaretti Crust** (page 18).

DRESSING IT UP
Whipped cream (flavored with a pinch of ground mace, if you like) and **Coffee Whipped Cream** (page 125) are both good spooned onto slices of this ice cream pie. **Mocha Sauce** (page 128) will intensify the coffee flavor. **Warm Chocolate Sauce** (page 126) flavored with almond liqueur is another way to go.

Chocolate-Almond-Ginger Ice Cream Pie

Makes one 9-inch pie; 6 to 8 servings

1. Combine the ice cream, almonds, chocolate, and ginger in a large mixing bowl and mash the mixture with the back of a wooden spoon until everything is well combined.

2. Turn the ice cream mixture into the prepared crust and smooth the top with the back of a spoon. Cover the pie with plastic wrap and freeze it until the filling is completely set, for at least 3 hours and up to 1 week.

Here's one of my favorite mix-in recipes. For an ice cream pie, it's surprisingly elegant. The almonds, white chocolate, and ginger really elevate a plain chocolate ice cream pie to dessert status. Crystallized ginger is available in natural food stores and in the spice section of many supermarkets.

2 pints chocolate ice cream, softened

½ cup almonds, coarsely chopped

4 ounces white chocolate, coarsely chopped

½ cup crystallized ginger, coarsely chopped

1 prepared crumb crust

CHOOSING A CRUST
Go with **Chocolate Cookie Crust** (page 13), **Oreo Cookie Crust** (page 14), or **Gingersnap Crust** (page 16).

DRESSING IT UP
Call me a glutton, but I think this pie looks and tastes undressed without both **Warm Chocolate Sauce** (page 126) and **Warm White Chocolate Sauce** (page 126).

Cookies and Cream Ice Cream Pie

Makes one 9-inch pie; 6 to 8 servings

2 pints any flavor ice cream, softened

2 cups coarsely chopped cookies

1 prepared crumb crust

1. Combine the ice cream and cookies in a large mixing bowl and mash the mixture with the back of a wooden spoon until the cookies and ice cream are well combined.

2. Turn the ice cream mixture into the prepared crust and smooth the top with the back of a spoon. Cover the pie with plastic wrap and freeze it until the filling is completely set, at least 3 hours and up to 1 week.

Cookies and ice cream are a classic combination, and together they make a wonderful pie filling. Try mint chip ice cream with chopped Oreos, coffee ice cream with almond biscotti, or peach ice cream with gingersnaps. Use homemade cookies or brownies for the ultimate cookies and cream ice cream pie.

CHOOSING A CRUST

Either match your crust with your cookies, or use **Sugar Cone Crust** (page 19) for an ice cream parlor flavor.

DRESSING IT UP

Toppings are a must. You've picked your ice cream and cookie flavors; now choose the accompaniments that will work with your choices.

Chocolate-Mint Sorbet Pie

Makes one 9-inch pie; 6 to 8 servings

Inspired by the manufacturer's claim that peppermint patties are low in fat, I decided to combine this delicious, creamy candy with nonfat chocolate sorbet. The result is a surprisingly rich-tasting pie.

1 pint chocolate sorbet, softened

12 miniature peppermint patties (about 5 ounces), chilled and coarsely chopped

1 prepared crumb crust

¾ cup heavy cream, chilled

6 tablespoons confectioners' sugar

⅛ teaspoon pure peppermint extract

1. Combine the sorbet and peppermint patties in a large mixing bowl and mash the mixture with the back of a wooden spoon until the peppermint patties and sorbet are well combined.

2. Turn the sorbet mixture into the prepared crust and smooth it with the back of a spoon. Place the pie in the freezer while you continue with the recipe.

3. Combine the heavy cream, confectioners' sugar, and peppermint extract in a medium-size mixing bowl and using an electric mixer beat the cream until it holds soft peaks. Remove the pie from the freezer and spread the whipped cream over the top with a rubber spatula. Cover the pie with plastic wrap and freeze it until the filling is completely set, at least 3 hours and up to 1 week.

CHOOSING A CRUST
Chocolate Cookie Crust (page 13) or **Oreo Cookie Crust** (page 14) adds another layer of chocolate flavor.

DRESSING IT UP
Serve **Hot Fudge Sauce** (page 127) on the side for anyone who isn't watching calories.

Cranberry and Butterscotch Chip Ice Cream Pie

Makes one 9-inch pie; 6 to 8 servings

1. Combine the ice cream, cranberries, and butterscotch chips in a large mixing bowl and mash the mixture with the back of a wooden spoon until all the ingredients are well combined.

2. Turn the ice cream mixture into the prepared crust and smooth the top with the back of a spoon. Cover the pie with plastic wrap and freeze it until the filling is completely set, at least 3 hours and up to 1 week.

Tart cranberries contrast wonderfully with sweet butterscotch chips in this simple mix-in pie.

2 pints vanilla ice cream, softened
¾ cup dried cranberries
¾ cup butterscotch chips
1 prepared crumb crust

CHOOSING A CRUST
Go with **Sugar Cone Crust** (page 19) or **Graham Cracker Crust** (page 11).

DRESSING IT UP
I love **Maple Walnut Sauce** (page 130) drizzled over slices of this pie. **Cranberry Dessert Sauce** (page 131) is a dressier option.

Caramel and Cinnamon Ice Cream Pie

Makes one 9-inch pie; 6 to 8 servings

2 pints vanilla ice cream, softened

1 teaspoon ground cinnamon

1 recipe Caramel Sauce (page 129),
    cooled to room temperature

1 prepared crumb crust

1. Combine the ice cream and cinnamon in a large mixing bowl and mash the ice cream with the back of a wooden spoon until the cinnamon and ice cream are well combined. Spoon half of the caramel sauce over the ice cream and fold it into the ice cream once or twice. Spoon the remaining caramel sauce over the ice cream and fold again. Be careful not to stir the ice cream too much or you will lose the thick ribbons of caramel.

2. Turn the ice cream mixture into the prepared crust and smooth the top with the back of a spoon. Cover the pie with plastic wrap and freeze it until the filling is completely set, at least 3 hours and up to 1 week.

To spice up plain vanilla ice cream, I'll often stir in a spoonful of cinnamon. Swirled with homemade caramel sauce, cinnamon ice cream makes a sensational pie.

CHOOSING A CRUST
Zwieback Crust (page 16) and **Graham Cracker Crust** (page 11) both complement the flavors of the pie.

DRESSING IT UP
This pie is wonderful served with sliced fresh peaches or plums on the side.

Trail Mix Pie

Makes one 9-inch pie; 6 to 8 servings

The name says it all. Raisins, peanuts, chocolate chips, coconut, and vanilla frozen yogurt combine to give this pie natural-tasting sweetness.

½ cup sweetened flaked coconut

2 pints vanilla frozen yogurt, softened

½ cup raisins

½ cup unsalted dry-roasted peanuts, coarsely chopped

¾ cup miniature semisweet chocolate chips

1 prepared crumb crust

1. Preheat the oven to 350 degrees. Place the coconut on a baking sheet and bake it until it is golden, stirring it once or twice, about 5 minutes. Watch the coconut carefully; it will go from golden to burned in an instant. Remove the pan from the oven and let the coconut cool completely.

2. Combine the frozen yogurt, raisins, peanuts, chocolate chips, and coconut in a large mixing bowl and mash the mixture with the back of a wooden spoon until everything is well combined.

3. Turn the yogurt mixture into the prepared crust and smooth the top with the back of a spoon. Cover the pie with plastic wrap and freeze it until the filling is completely set, for at least 3 hours and up to 1 week.

CHOOSING A CRUST
Graham Cracker and Oatmeal Crumb Crust (page 13) will add more wholesome ingredients to this dessert.

DRESSING IT UP
Chocolate Peanut Butter Sauce (page 128) is yummy here, as is **Chocolate Coconut Sauce** (page 129). Plain **Hot Fudge Sauce** (page 127) wouldn't be bad either.

Peanut Butter Cup Pie

Makes one 9-inch pie; 6 to 8 servings

1. Combine the ice cream and peanut butter cups in a large mixing bowl and mash the mixture with the back of a wooden spoon until the peanut butter cups and ice cream are well combined.

2. Turn the ice cream mixture into the prepared crust and smooth it with the back of a spoon. Place the pie in the freezer while you continue with the recipe.

3. Combine the heavy cream, confectioners' sugar, and vanilla in a medium-size mixing bowl and using an electric mixer whip the cream until it holds soft peaks. Remove the pie from the freezer and spread the whipped cream over the top with a rubber spatula. Cover the pie with plastic wrap and freeze it until the filling is completely set, at least 3 hours and up to 1 week.

When I serve them store-bought peanut butter cup ice cream, my children always complain that there's too much ice cream and not enough peanut butter cup. I wanted to make an ice cream pie with so many peanut butter cups mixed in that the kids wouldn't have to poke around to find the candy. This pie contains the proper ratio of ice cream to candy. I guarantee that you will get a taste of peanut butter cup with every bite.

1 pint vanilla ice cream, softened

20 miniature peanut butter cups (about 5 ounces), chilled and coarsely chopped

1 prepared crumb crust

¾ cup heavy cream, chilled

6 tablespoons confectioners' sugar

1 teaspoon pure vanilla extract

CHOOSING A CRUST
Sugar Cone Crust (page 19) or **Graham Cracker Crust** (page 11) is best with this pie.

DRESSING IT UP
Hot Fudge Sauce (page 127) is great here, as is **Chocolate Peanut Butter Sauce** (page 128).

Mango and Coconut Ice Cream Pie

Makes one 9-inch pie; 6 to 8 servings

1 cup sweetened flaked coconut

1 pint vanilla ice cream, softened

½ teaspoon pure coconut extract

1 prepared crumb crust

1 pint mango sorbet, softened

1. Preheat the oven to 350 degrees. Place the coconut on a baking sheet and bake it until it is golden, stirring it once or twice, about 5 minutes. Watch the coconut carefully; it will go from golden to burned in an instant. Remove the pan from the oven and let the coconut cool completely.

2. Combine the ice cream, coconut, and coconut extract in a large mixing bowl and mash the ice cream with the back of a wooden spoon until all the ingredients are well combined.

3. Turn half of the coconut ice cream mixture into the prepared crust and smooth the top with the back of a spoon. Spread half of the mango sorbet over the ice cream. Repeat with the remaining ice cream and then the sorbet. Cover the pie with plastic wrap and freeze it until the filling is completely set, at least 3 hours and up to 1 week.

The tropical flavors of this pie make it a perfect summer dessert.

CHOOSING A CRUST

Graham Cracker Crust (page 11) and **Graham Cracker and Coconut Crust** (page 12) are good choices.

DRESSING IT UP

Warm **Caramel Sauce** (page 129) made with rum is very good with this pie.

Raspberry and Lemon Frozen Yogurt Pie

Makes one 9-inch pie; 6 to 8 servings

1 pint raspberry frozen yogurt, thawed

1 cup fresh raspberries or frozen raspberries, thawed

1 prepared crumb crust

1 pint lemon sorbet, softened

1. Combine the frozen yogurt and raspberries in a large mixing bowl and mash the frozen yogurt with the back of a wooden spoon until the raspberries and frozen yogurt are well combined.

2. Turn half of the frozen yogurt mixture into the prepared crust and smooth the top with the back of a spoon. Spread half of the lemon sorbet over the ice cream. Repeat with the remaining frozen yogurt and then the sorbet. Cover the pie with plastic wrap and freeze it until the filling is completely set, at least 3 hours and up to 1 week.

This is a wonderfully refreshing and relatively lowfat summer dessert. Raspberry frozen yogurt gets a flavor boost with the addition of fresh or frozen raspberries.

CHOOSING A CRUST

Vanilla Wafer Crust (page 17) and **Lemon Nut Cookie Crust** (page 19) are just right with raspberries and lemon.

DRESSING IT UP

To keep this dessert relatively spare, use a few fresh raspberries and mint leaves as garnish. Going in the other direction, whipped cream and **Raspberry Mash** (page 130) up the luxury quotient.

Peach Sorbet and Blueberry Ice Cream Pie

Makes one 9-inch pie; 6 to 8 servings

1. Combine the frozen yogurt and blueberries in a large mixing bowl and mash the frozen yogurt with the back of a wooden spoon until the blueberries and frozen yogurt are well combined.

2. Turn half of the frozen yogurt mixture into the prepared crust and smooth the top with the back of a spoon. Spread half of the peach sorbet over the frozen yogurt. Repeat with the remaining frozen yogurt and then the sorbet. Cover the pie with plastic wrap and freeze it until the filling is completely set, at least 3 hours and up to 1 week.

Here's a simple frozen yogurt and sorbet combination that's perfect at the end of a summer barbecue.

1 pint vanilla frozen yogurt, softened

1 cup fresh blueberries, picked over for stems, or frozen blueberries, thawed

1 prepared crumb crust

1 pint peach sorbet, softened

CHOOSING A CRUST
You can't go wrong with **Graham Cracker Crust** (page 11). **Zwieback Crust** (page 16) is another tasty option.

DRESSING IT UP
Whipped cream and **Maple Walnut Sauce** (page 130) dress up slices of this pie beautifully.

Pistachio and Orange Ice Cream Pie

Makes one 9-inch pie; 6 to 8 servings

1 pint pistachio ice cream, softened

1 prepared crumb crust

1 pint orange sorbet, softened

1. Spoon half of the pistachio ice cream into the prepared crust and smooth the top with the back of a wooden spoon. Spread half of the orange sorbet over the ice cream. Repeat with the remaining ice cream and then the sorbet.

2. Cover the pie with plastic wrap and freeze it until the filling is completely set, at least 3 hours and up to 1 week.

This is barely a recipe—just a pint of ice cream, a pint of sorbet, and a crumb crust. But because pistachios and oranges have such an affinity for each other, this pie is much more than the sum of its parts—especially when it is served with Warm White Chocolate Sauce on the side.

CHOOSING A CRUST
Sugar Cone Crust (page 19) is just right here. **Graham Cracker Crust** (page 11) works, too.

DRESSING IT UP
Warm White Chocolate Sauce (page 126) and a shower of coarsely chopped **Sugared Pistachio Nuts** (page 132) turn this simple pie into an event.

Strawberry-Almond Heath Bar Ice Cream Pie

Makes one 9-inch pie; 6 to 8 servings

1 pint strawberry ice cream, softened

1 prepared crumb crust

1 cup almond toffee bits

1 cup heavy cream, chilled

½ cup confectioners' sugar

½ teaspoon pure almond extract

1. Spread half of the ice cream across the bottom of the prepared crust, smoothing the top with a rubber spatula. Sprinkle ½ cup of the almond toffee bits evenly over the ice cream. Repeat with the remaining ice cream and then the toffee bits. Place the ice cream pie in the freezer while you continue with the recipe.

Toffee bits give ice cream pies great flavor and texture. They are sold in the baking aisle of the supermarket alongside chocolate chips. I love the almond variety sprinkled over strawberry ice cream.

2. Combine the heavy cream, confectioners' sugar, and almond extract in a medium-size mixing bowl and using an electric mixer whip the cream until it holds soft peaks. Remove the pie from the freezer and spread the whipped cream over the top with a rubber spatula. Cover the pie with plastic wrap and freeze it until the filling is completely set, at least 3 hours and up to 1 week.

CHOOSING A CRUST

This pie has got some strong flavors and textures already, so I go with a neutral **Sugar Cone Crust** (page 19).

DRESSING IT UP

Strawberry Mash (page 130) completes this pie. Or just garnish slices with a few fresh strawberries.

Coffee Heath Bar Ice Cream Pie

Makes one 9-inch pie; 6 to 8 servings

Although you can buy coffee ice cream with bits of milk-chocolate-covered toffee bits already stirred in, if you make your own blend, you can add so much more candy! Frozen chocolate whipped cream makes a simple, delicious topping.

1. Combine the ice cream and toffee bits in a large mixing bowl and mash the ice cream with the back of a wooden spoon until the toffee bits and ice cream are well combined.

2. Turn the ice cream mixture into the prepared crust and smooth the top with the back of a spoon. Place the pie in the freezer while you continue with the recipe.

3. Combine the heavy cream, confectioners' sugar, cocoa powder, and espresso powder in a medium-size mixing bowl and using an electric mixer whip the cream until it holds soft peaks. Remove the pie from the freezer and spread the whipped cream over the top with a rubber spatula. Cover the pie with plastic wrap and freeze it until the filling is completely set, at least 3 hours and up to 1 week.

1 pint coffee ice cream, softened

1½ cups milk chocolate–covered toffee bits (one 8-ounce bag)

1 prepared crumb crust

1 cup heavy cream, chilled

¼ cup confectioners' sugar

¼ cup unsweetened cocoa powder

1 tablespoon espresso powder

CHOOSING A CRUST
Sugar Cone Crust (page 19), **Chocolate Cookie Crust** (page 13), or **Oreo Cookie Crust** (page 14) does the trick here.

DRESSING IT UP
If you must have something warm to top your ice cream, try **Chocolate Caramel Sauce** (page 127).

Banana Split Ice Cream Pie

Makes one 9-inch pie; 6 to 8 servings

2 small ripe bananas, peeled

1 tablespoon fresh lemon juice

1 pint vanilla ice cream, softened

1 prepared crumb crust

1 recipe Caramel Sauce (page 129), cooled to room temperature

½ cup walnut pieces

1 cup heavy cream, chilled

½ cup confectioners' sugar

½ teaspoon pure vanilla extract

1 recipe Hot Fudge Sauce (page 127)

6 to 8 maraschino cherries

1. Place the bananas in a large mixing bowl, sprinkle them with the lemon juice, and mash them lightly with a fork. Add the ice cream and mash the mixture with the back of a wooden spoon until the ice cream and bananas are well combined.

2. Turn the ice cream mixture into the prepared crust and smooth the top with the back of a spoon. Spread the Caramel Sauce over the ice cream and sprinkle on the walnuts. Place the pie in the freezer while you continue with the recipe.

3. Combine the heavy cream, confectioners' sugar, and vanilla in a medium-size mixing bowl and using an electric mixer whip the cream until it holds soft peaks. Remove the pie from the freezer and spread the whipped cream over the top with a rubber spatula. Cover the pie with plastic wrap and freeze it until the filling is completely set, at least 3 hours and up to 1 week.

4. To serve, cut the pie into 6 or 8 slices and place each slice on a dessert plate. Pour some Hot Fudge Sauce over each slice and top with a maraschino cherry.

This is just what it sounds like— a banana split in a pie shell.

CHOOSING A CRUST
Sugar Cone Crust (page 19) reinforces the ice cream parlor flavors here. **Graham Cracker Crust** (page 11) is also good.

DRESSING IT UP
There's no need to embellish this one.

Cherry and Chocolate Chunk Ice Cream Pie

Makes one 9-inch pie; 6 to 8 servings

1. Combine the ice cream, cherries, and chocolate in a large mixing bowl and mash the ice cream with the back of a wooden spoon until all the ingredients are well combined.

2. Turn the ice cream mixture into the prepared crust and smooth the top with the back of a spoon. Place the pie in the freezer while you continue with the recipe.

3. Combine the heavy cream, confectioners' sugar, and Kirsch in a medium-size mixing bowl and using an electric mixer whip the cream until it holds soft peaks. Remove the pie from the freezer and spread the whipped cream over the top with a rubber spatula. Cover the pie with plastic wrap and freeze it until the filling is completely set, for at least 3 hours and up to 1 week.

1 pint chocolate ice cream, softened

1½ cups fresh cherries, pitted and coarsely chopped, or 1½ cups frozen pitted cherries, thawed

3½ ounces bittersweet chocolate, coarsely chopped

1 prepared crumb crust

¾ cup heavy cream, chilled

6 tablespoons confectioners' sugar

1 tablespoon Kirsch

Who doesn't love the combination of chocolate and cherries? A topping of Kirsch-flavored whipped cream adds a layer of luxury.

CHOOSING A CRUST
Chocolate Cookie Crust (page 13) is called for here.

DRESSING IT UP
Warm Chocolate Sauce (page 126) flavored with Kirsch nicely finishes slices of this pie.

S'Mores Pie

Makes one 9-inch pie; 6 to 8 servings

2 pints chocolate, vanilla, or coffee ice cream, softened

3½ ounces milk chocolate, such as Hershey's, broken into ½-inch squares

1 prepared crumb crust

1½ cups Marshmallow Fluff

1 recipe Hot Fudge Sauce (page 127)

2 whole graham crackers, each one broken into 4 pieces along the serrations

1. Combine the ice cream and chocolate in a large mixing bowl and mash the ice cream with the back of a wooden spoon until the chocolate pieces and ice cream are well combined.

2. Turn the ice cream mixture into the prepared crust and smooth the top with the back of a spoon. Cover the pie with plastic wrap and freeze it until the filling is completely set, at least 3 hours and up to 1 week.

3. Just before serving, spread the Marshmallow Fluff across the top of the pie. Place slices on dessert plates. Drizzle each slice with Hot Fudge Sauce and garnish each slice with a piece of graham cracker.

Choose whatever flavor of ice cream you like best to fill this pie. Given the graham crackers, hot fudge, and Marshmallow Fluff, the flavor ice cream you use is almost beside the point. Fluff is sticky and can be difficult to spread. I find that a large metal offset spatula, used with a firm hand, does the trick.

CHOOSING A CRUST
It wouldn't be S'Mores without a **Graham Cracker Crust** (page 11).

DRESSING IT UP
Just have extra hot fudge on hand for anyone who wants seconds.

I Can't Believe It's an Icebox Pie

Fresh Raspberry and Blueberry Pie

Blueberry Icebox Pie

Strawberry-Rhubarb Icebox Pie

Fig and Walnut Pie

Maple-Pecan Icebox Pie

Icebox Dream Pie

Chocolate-Almond Icebox Pie

Nobody loves icebox pie more than I do. But after preparing dozens of mousse pies, pudding pies, and ice cream pies, I began to crave "real" pie for a change. You know what I'm talking about—sweet and tart strawberry-rhubarb pie, blueberry pie with whole berries, the kind of sticky pecan pie that dentists hate. I wondered if there were ways to make these pies without baking, so I began experimenting with simple stovetop pie fillings that would satisfy my craving without the need for a lot of work. The following recipes are the result. Use them when you want to serve a juicy fruit pie or chewy nut pie but don't want to turn on the oven. Each one is easy in the extreme and utterly satisfying.

Fruit pies are especially simple. If you've got perfectly ripe berries on hand, one of the quickest ways to turn them into pie is to mix them gently with some warm jam and pour them into a crumb crust. The sticky jam adds a little bit of sweetness and holds the fruit together well enough so you can slice the pie. Or thicken fruit with cornstarch on top of the stove, pour the filling into a crumb crust, and refrigerate the pie until after dinner. This type of fruit pie has the refreshingly slippery texture of pudding pie but is light rather than rich.

Nut pies are among my absolute favorites, so I was especially excited about the great results I got from filling pie shells with a few different nut mixtures I cooked up in a saucepan.

Quick nut candy also makes satisfyingly chewy pie filling. I've included two versions here. Fig and Walnut Pie is filled with a mixture of chopped dried fruit and nuts sweetened and held together with melted brown sugar and corn syrup and spiced with a little cinnamon. In Chocolate-Almond Icebox Pie, the nuts are held together by gooey chocolate caramel. Yum.

Fresh Raspberry and Blueberry Pie

Makes one 9-inch pie; 6 to 8 servings

1. Combine the berries in a large mixing bowl.

2. Place the jam in a small saucepan and heat it over medium heat until it is simmering. Remove the pot from the heat and stir in the lemon juice. Pour the hot jam over the berries and toss them gently to coat.

3. Scrape the berry mixture into the prepared crust. Cover the pie with plastic wrap and refrigerate it until the filling is completely set, at least 3 hours and up to 6 hours.

3 cups fresh raspberries

3 cups fresh blueberries, picked over for stems

1 cup seedless raspberry jam

2 teaspoons fresh lemon juice

1 prepared crumb crust

Raspberry jam does double duty here: sweetening fresh berries and binding them together. Use only fresh fruit that is perfectly dry; frozen berries will make the pie soggy. This pie is best served the day it is made.

CHOOSING A CRUST
Graham Cracker Crust (page 11) is good with fresh berries; **Lemon Nut Cookie Crust** (page 19) and **Amaretti Crust** (page 18) are also lovely.

DRESSING IT UP
Whipped cream is a natural accompaniment for fresh berries.

Blueberry Icebox Pie

Makes one 9-inch pie; 6 to 8 servings

¼ cup cornstarch

¼ cup water

5 cups fresh blueberries, picked over for stems, or 5 cups frozen blueberries, thawed

⅔ cup sugar

½ teaspoon ground cinnamon

¼ teaspoon ground nutmeg

1 tablespoon unsalted butter

1 prepared crumb crust

1. Combine the cornstarch and water in a small bowl and stir the mixture until it is smooth.

2. Combine 3 cups of the blueberries, the sugar, cinnamon, and nutmeg in a medium-size saucepan. Bring the pot to a boil, stirring occasionally. Stir in the cornstarch mixture and cook the mixture over medium heat, stirring constantly, until it is thickened. Cook an additional 2 minutes. Remove the pot from the heat and stir in the butter and remaining 2 cups blueberries.

3. Scrape the filling into the prepared crust. Cover the pie with plastic wrap and refrigerate it until the filling is completely set, at least 6 hours and up to 1 day.

This cool and refreshing pie is a wonderful alternative to traditional blueberry pie, especially on hot summer days. The fruit filling is thickened with cornstarch on top of the stove, poured into a crumb crust, and chilled until well set. The finished pie has a firm but pleasing consistency and cuts beautifully.

CHOOSING A CRUST
Graham Cracker and Oatmeal Crumb Crust (page 13) or **Graham Cracker and Nut Crust** (page 11) would both taste great.

DRESSING IT UP
Whipped cream is my choice with this version of blueberry pie.

Strawberry-Rhubarb Icebox Pie

Makes one 9-inch pie; 6 to 8 servings

¼ cup cornstarch

¾ cup water

¾ cup sugar

4½ cups stringed and chopped rhubarb stalks (about 1¼ pounds), or one 20-ounce bag frozen chopped rhubarb

2 cups fresh strawberries, hulled, or frozen strawberries, thawed

1 tablespoon unsalted butter

1 teaspoon pure vanilla extract

1 prepared crumb crust

1. Combine the cornstarch and ¼ cup of the water in a small bowl and stir until the mixture is smooth.

2. Combine the sugar, rhubarb, and the remaining ½ cup water in a medium-size saucepan. Bring the pot to a boil. Reduce the heat to medium-low and simmer the rhubarb until it is soft and falling apart and most of the water has evaporated, 5 to 7 minutes. Stir in the cornstarch mixture and cook, stirring constantly, over medium heat until the mixture is thickened. Cook an additional 2 minutes. Remove the pot from the heat and stir in the strawberries, butter, and vanilla

3. Scrape the mixture into the prepared crust. Cover the pie with plastic wrap and refrigerate it until the filling is completely set, at least 6 hours and up to 1 day.

This icebox version of classic strawberry-rhubarb pie couldn't be simpler, especially if you use frozen fruit that's already been prepared and just has to be dumped into the pot. The strawberries are stirred in at the last minute, so they stay firm and give the pie some texture.

CHOOSING A CRUST
Sweet **Vanilla Wafer Crust** (page 17) is just right with this slightly tart filling. **Zwieback Crust** (page 16), with its mild spiciness, is also a good choice.

DRESSING IT UP
A little vanilla ice cream on the side isn't necessary, but it would be delicious.

Fig and Walnut Pie

Makes one 9-inch pie; 6 to 8 servings

1. Combine the butter, brown sugar, and corn syrup in a medium-size saucepan and bring the pot to a boil. Boil the mixture for 1 minute. Stir in the figs, walnuts, heavy cream, and cinnamon and bring the pot back to a boil. Reduce the heat to medium and simmer the mixture for 5 minutes.

2. Scrape the hot filling into the prepared crust and let the filling cool to room temperature. Cover the pie with plastic wrap and refrigerate it until the filling is completely set, at least 3 hours and up to 3 days.

This unusual pie filled with dried fruit and nuts is sweet but sophisticated. I like it in the winter after a simple dinner of pasta and salad.

½ cup (1 stick) unsalted butter

¼ cup firmly packed light brown sugar

6 tablespoons light corn syrup

1½ cups dried figs (about 10 ounces), stemmed and quartered

1½ cups walnuts, coarsely chopped

¼ cup heavy cream

½ teaspoon ground cinnamon

1 prepared crumb crust

CHOOSING A CRUST
Graham Cracker Crust (page 11), with its coarse texture, stands up well to this chunky filling.

DRESSING IT UP
I like figs with coffee and/or chocolate. Serve slices of this pie with small scoops of coffee or chocolate ice cream. Warm **Mocha Sauce** (page 128) is also delicious.

Maple-Pecan Icebox Pie

Makes one 9-inch pie; 6 to 8 servings

¾ cup (1½ sticks) unsalted butter

¾ cup firmly packed light brown sugar

¼ cup light corn syrup

¼ cup pure maple syrup

3 tablespoons heavy cream

3 cups pecan halves

1 prepared crumb crust

1. Combine the butter, brown sugar, corn syrup, and maple syrup in a medium-size saucepan and bring the pot to a boil, stirring the mixture frequently with a wooden spoon. Stir in the heavy cream and pecan halves and let the pot return to a boil. Reduce the heat to medium and cook the mixture at a lively simmer (not a rolling boil), stirring occasionally, for 12 minutes.

2. Remove the pot from the heat and scrape the hot filling into the prepared crust. Let the filling cool to room temperature. Cover the pie with plastic wrap and refrigerate it until the filling is completely set, at least 3 hours and up to 1 day.

Here is a wonderfully sweet and sticky confection for anyone who craves pecan pie.

CHOOSING A CRUST
I like **Graham Cracker Crust** (page 11) with this filling.

DRESSING IT UP
A little bit of whipped cream looks nice and tastes great on top of each slice.

Icebox Dream Pie

Makes one 9-inch pie; 6 to 8 servings

This pie was inspired by a venerable recipe published on the back of Eagle brand sweetened condensed milk cans. The milk holds together a mixture of nuts, coconut, and dried apricots. Chocolate chips sprinkled on top of the hot filling melt and are smoothed with a spatula to become a simple icing.

1½ cups pecans, coarsely chopped

1 cup sweetened flaked coconut

One 14-ounce can sweetened condensed milk

1 cup dried apricots, coarsely chopped

1 prepared crumb crust

1½ cups semisweet or milk chocolate chips

1. Combine the pecans and coconut in a medium-size saucepan and cook over medium-high heat, stirring occasionally, until the coconut just begins to brown, 5 to 7 minutes. Stir in the sweetened condensed milk and bring the mixture to a boil. Reduce the heat to medium-low and simmer for 1 minute. Remove the pot from the heat and stir in the apricots.

2. Scrape the mixture into the prepared crust and smooth the top with a rubber spatula.

3. Sprinkle the chocolate chips over the hot filling and smooth the chocolate chips with a clean rubber spatula until they are melted and form an icing. Let the filling cool to room temperature. Cover the pie with plastic wrap and refrigerate it until the filling is completely set, at least 3 hours and up to 3 days.

CHOOSING A CRUST
Graham Cracker Crust (page 11) is best here.

DRESSING IT UP
This pie is complete in and of itself.

Chocolate-Almond Icebox Pie

Makes one 9-inch pie; 6 to 8 servings

1. Combine the butter, brown sugar, and corn syrup in a medium-size saucepan and bring the pot to a boil, stirring frequently with a wooden spoon. Stir in the heavy cream and almonds and let the pot return to a boil. Reduce the heat to medium and cook the mixture at a lively simmer (not a rolling boil), stirring occasionally, for 12 minutes.

2. Remove the pot from the heat, add the chocolate, and stir until it is completely melted.

3. Scrape the hot filling into the prepared crust. Let the filling cool to room temperature. Cover the pie with plastic wrap and refrigerate it until the filling is completely set, at least 3 hours and up to 1 day.

This pie features a very simple candy filling poured into a crumb crust and allowed to cool so that it's wonderfully chewy, like chocolate caramel.

¾ cup (1½ sticks) unsalted butter

¾ cup firmly packed dark brown sugar

½ cup light corn syrup

3 tablespoons heavy cream

3 cups whole almonds, coarsely chopped

2½ ounces unsweetened chocolate, coarsely chopped

1 prepared crumb crust

CHOOSING A CRUST
Oreo Cookie Crust (page 14) is delicious with this gooey candy filling.

DRESSING IT UP
Lighten up slices of this pie with small scoops of vanilla or coffee ice cream.

Dressing It Up

Whipped Cream

Coffee Whipped Cream

Honey Whipped Cream

Warm Chocolate Sauce

Warm White Chocolate Sauce

Hot Fudge Sauce

Chocolate Caramel Sauce

Chocolate Peanut Butter Sauce

Mocha Sauce

Chocolate Coconut Sauce

Caramel Sauce

Maple Walnut Sauce

Berry Mash

Cranberry Dessert Sauce

Raspberry Coulis

Mango Coulis

Sugared Nuts

Nougatine

Put a slice of pie on a dessert plate and chances are it will look a little lonely. Does it seem to be calling out for whipped cream? Chocolate sauce? Macerated berries? All three? This chapter supplies the recipes you need to heed that call, in much less time than you might think. Icebox pie presented with all the trimmings is pretty spectacular. Nobody has to know that making it is not as hard as it looks.

Considering that the pie recipes themselves are relatively simple, it would be ridiculous to sweat over the accompaniments. The toppings and sauces that follow are all quick and easy to make. With the exception of whipped cream, which is best served on the day it is made, all of them will keep in the refrigerator or freezer for at least a week. So if you can't decide between the whipped cream, chocolate sauce, and berries, you can go ahead and make all three.

In general, I like toppings that enhance the flavors of the pie filling and provide some textural contrast. I've come up with a few guidelines that help me match pies with accompaniments:

- Follow the "same but different" principle. For example, when topping an Orange and Spice Pie made with orange zest, use whipped cream made with orange liqueur instead of more zest. White Chocolate and Raspberry Pie, made with whole raspberries, gets a different kind of raspberry kick from smooth, seedless Raspberry Coulis.

- Lighten up. Fluffy whipped cream is great on top of very dense fillings such as chocolate pudding or ice cream with dates and almonds mixed in.

- Pies that have already got whipped cream folded into the filling are usually better with thicker, heavier sauces. Lemon Cream Pie, for exam-

ple, doesn't need more whipped cream on top. It's better with chunks of fresh fruit or a fruit sauce. Bring fluffy Marshmallow Pie down to earth by drizzling Chocolate Peanut Butter Sauce over each slice.

- Warm sauces are wonderful on frozen pies. The contrast between warm and cold brings out the best in both components.

- Add some crunch. Is your smooth and creamy icebox pie a little too comforting? A sprinkling of chopped Nougatine will add interest to Papaya Mousse Pie. Chopped Sugared Pistachios give Pistachio and Orange Ice Cream Pie some needed texture.

I've made specific suggestions for matching pies with accompaniments at the end of each recipe, but feel free to mix and match according to your own taste.

Although I make exceptions, I like to top icebox pie after I've sliced it. I'll put a dollop of whipped cream on each serving, pour some chocolate sauce over the whipped cream, and sprinkle some nuts

on top. This way, I can put as much or as little of a particular topping on a particular slice as I like, honoring requests for extra hot fudge or no pecans. Certain icebox pies, like Chocolate Pudding Pie and Banana Cream Pie, are traditionally covered with whipped cream before they are sliced. You can either follow tradition or break with it, depending on what's easier and what works better for you and your guests.

I designed the following recipes with pie in mind, but I've found that many of them are fantastic over plain ice cream. More often than not, on a busy weeknight I'll find myself skipping the pie altogether and spooning some warm Maple Walnut Sauce over coffee Häagen-Dazs, or drizzling Chocolate Peanut Butter Sauce over French vanilla. My friends and family still feel treated, even if I haven't brought a pie to the table.

Whipped Cream

Makes enough to top 1 pie

Many icebox pies just cry out for a topping of whipped cream. I sweeten my whipped cream with quick-dissolving confectioners' sugar and flavor it with vanilla and sometimes a little liqueur, depending on the type of pie I'm serving.

1 cup heavy cream, chilled

2 tablespoons confectioners' sugar

1 teaspoon pure vanilla extract

1 tablespoon Kahlua, Grand Marnier, framboise, Calvados, Frangelico, or any other liqueur of your choice (optional)

Combine the heavy cream, confectioners' sugar, vanilla, and liqueur, if you are using it, in a medium-size mixing bowl. Using an electric mixer fitted with a whisk attachment whip the cream on high speed until it just holds stiff peaks. Do not overwhip it. Whipped Cream will keep, covered with plastic wrap and refrigerated, for up to 6 hours. Whisk the whipped cream for a couple of seconds before using it.

Coffee Whipped Cream

Makes enough to top 1 pie

Coffee-flavored whipped cream complements many chocolate-flavored pies.

1 cup heavy cream

2 tablespoons confectioners' sugar

1½ teaspoons instant espresso powder

1 teaspoon pure vanilla extract

Combine the heavy cream, confectioners' sugar, espresso powder, and vanilla in a medium-size mixing bowl. Using an electric mixer fitted with a whisk attachment whip the cream on high speed until it just holds stiff peaks. Do not overwhip it. Coffee Whipped Cream will keep, covered with plastic wrap and refrigerated, for up to 6 hours. Whisk the whipped cream for a couple of seconds before using it.

Honey Whipped Cream

Makes enough to top 1 pie

Whipped cream sweetened with honey adds an extra flavor dimension to many fruit pies. Specialty honeys such as clover and orange blossom are especially delicious in whipped cream, although any honey will do.

1 cup heavy cream

1 tablespoon plus 1 teaspoon honey

⅛ teaspoon ground cinnamon (optional)

Combine the heavy cream, honey, and cinnamon, if you are using it, in a medium-size mixing bowl. Using an electric mixer fitted with a whisk attachment whip the cream on high speed until the cream just holds stiff peaks. Do not overwhip it. Honey Whipped Cream will keep, covered with plastic wrap and refrigerated, for up to 6 hours. Whisk the whipped cream for a couple of seconds before using it.

Warm Chocolate Sauce

Makes ¾ cup, enough to accompany 1 pie

Flavor this simple chocolate sauce with whichever liqueur complements your pie.

8 ounces bittersweet chocolate, finely chopped

¼ cup water

1 tablespoon hazelnut, almond, orange, raspberry, or coffee liqueur (optional)

1. Put 2 inches of water in a medium-size saucepan and bring the pot to a bare simmer.

2. Combine the chocolate and ¼ cup water in a stainless-steel bowl big enough to rest on top of the saucepan and place the bowl over the simmering water, making sure that the water doesn't touch the bottom of the bowl. Heat the chocolate, whisking occasionally, until it is completely melted. Turn off the heat. Stir in the liqueur, if you are using it. Warm Chocolate Sauce will keep, refrigerated in an airtight container, for up to 2 days. Reheat the sauce in the microwave for 1½ minutes or over a pot of simmering water.

Warm White Chocolate Sauce

Makes about 1 cup, enough to accompany 1 pie

For the best sauce, use a premium brand of white chocolate such as Lindt or Ghirardelli, both of which contain a generous amount of cocoa butter. White chocolate is temperamental; heat it very gently over barely simmering water for a smooth, not grainy, consistency.

6 ounces white chocolate, finely chopped

¼ cup (½ stick) unsalted butter, cut into small pieces

¼ cup heavy cream

1. Put 2 inches of water in a medium-size saucepan and bring the pot to a bare simmer.

2. Combine the chocolate, butter, and heavy cream in a stainless-steel bowl big enough to rest on top of the saucepan and place the bowl over the simmering water, making sure that the water doesn't touch the bottom of the bowl. Heat the chocolate, whisking occasionally, until it is just melted. Warm White Chocolate Sauce will keep, refrigerated in an airtight container, for up to 1 week. Reheat the sauce in the microwave for 1½ minutes or over a pot of simmering water.

Hot Fudge Sauce

Makes about 1½ cups, enough to accompany 1 pie, with some left over

For delicately textured icebox pies, I use Warm Chocolate Sauce. Hot Fudge Sauce is best on sturdier frozen desserts. When poured over a slice of ice cream pie, this fudge sauce hardens to the consistency of chewy chocolate taffy.

¼ cup sugar

2 tablespoons unsweetened cocoa powder

¾ cup heavy cream

½ cup light corn syrup

2 ounces bittersweet chocolate, coarsely chopped

2 tablespoons unsalted butter

1 teaspoon pure vanilla extract

⅛ teaspoon salt

1. Combine the sugar, cocoa powder, heavy cream, and corn syrup in a heavy medium-size saucepan and whisk to combine. Add the chocolate and bring the pot to a boil over medium-high heat, whisking constantly. Reduce the heat to medium-low and gently boil the sauce, without stirring, for 5 minutes.

2. Remove the pot from the heat and stir in the butter, vanilla, and salt. Hot Fudge Sauce will keep, refrigerated in an airtight container, for up to 2 weeks. Reheat the sauce in a saucepan over medium-low heat, or in a microwave for 1½ minutes, before serving.

Chocolate Caramel Sauce

Makes about 1¼ cups, enough to accompany 1 pie

Chocolate Caramel Sauce is thicker and richer than Warm Chocolate Sauce, but not quite as gooey as Hot Fudge Sauce.

½ cup sugar

2 tablespoons water

1 cup heavy cream

3½ ounces bittersweet chocolate, finely chopped

1 teaspoon pure vanilla extract

Pinch of salt

1. Combine the sugar and water in a small saucepan. Bring the pot to a boil and cook the mixture until it turns a light amber color. Do not stir. If part of the syrup is turning darker than the rest of the syrup, gently tilt the pan to even out the cooking.

2. As soon as the syrup is a uniform amber color, stir in the heavy cream with a long-handled wooden spoon. The mixture will bubble up. Remove the pot from the heat and stir in the chocolate until it melts and blends into the sauce. Pour the sauce through a fine mesh strainer into an airtight container. Stir in the vanilla and salt. Chocolate Caramel Sauce will keep, refrigerated in an airtight container, for up to 2 weeks. Reheat the sauce in the microwave for 1½ minutes or on the stovetop until it is warm and pourable.

Chocolate Peanut Butter Sauce

Makes about 1 cup, enough to accompany 1 pie

If you love the combination of chocolate and peanut butter, this is the dessert sauce for you.

1 tablespoon firmly packed light brown sugar

1 tablespoon light corn syrup

¼ cup smooth peanut butter

½ cup heavy cream

3½ ounces bittersweet chocolate, finely chopped

Pinch of salt

2 tablespoons water

1. Combine the brown sugar, corn syrup, peanut butter, and heavy cream in a heavy medium-size saucepan and bring the pot to a boil over medium heat, whisking constantly.

2. Remove the pot from the heat and whisk in the chocolate, salt, and water until the chocolate melts and the sauce is smooth. Chocolate Peanut Butter Sauce will keep, refrigerated in an airtight container, for up to 2 weeks. Reheat the sauce in the microwave for 1½ minutes or on the stovetop until it is warm and pourable.

Mocha Sauce

Makes about 1 cup, enough to accompany 1 pie

A generous amount of instant espresso powder gives this chocolate sauce a bitter edge that balances the sweetness of many icebox pies.

½ cup firmly packed light brown sugar

2 tablespoons light corn syrup

2 tablespoons instant espresso powder

1 tablespoon unsalted butter

2 ounces unsweetened chocolate, finely chopped

½ cup heavy cream

1 tablespoon coffee liqueur

1. Combine the brown sugar, corn syrup, espresso powder, and butter in a heavy medium-size saucepan and bring the pot to a boil. Continue to boil the mixture, stirring constantly, for 1 minute.

2. Remove the pot from the heat and stir in the chocolate and heavy cream until the chocolate melts and the sauce is smooth. Pour the sauce through a fine mesh strainer and into an airtight container. Stir in the coffee liqueur. Let the sauce cool slightly. Mocha Sauce will keep, refrigerated in an airtight container, for up to 1 week. Reheat the sauce in the microwave for 1½ minutes or on the stovetop before serving.

Chocolate Coconut Sauce

Makes about 1¾ cups, enough to accompany 1 pie, with some left over

Cream of coconut adds sweetness as well as richness and coconut flavor to this easy-to-make sauce. Chocolate Coconut Sauce is good on tropical fruit pies and many ice cream pies.

One 15-ounce can cream of coconut, such as Coco Lopez

6 tablespoons unsweetened cocoa powder

½ teaspoon pure vanilla extract

½ teaspoon pure coconut extract

Pinch of salt

1. Combine the cream of coconut and cocoa powder in a medium-size saucepan and heat the mixture over medium-low, whisking occasionally, until the cocoa powder is dissolved and the sauce is smooth.

2. Remove the pot from the heat and stir in the vanilla, coconut extract, and salt. Chocolate Coconut Sauce will keep in an airtight container at room temperature for up to 3 days. Reheat the sauce in the microwave for 1½ minutes or on the stovetop and whisk before serving.

Caramel Sauce

Makes about 1 cup, enough to accompany 1 pie

The rum is optional here, but I like the way it tempers the sweetness of cream-enriched caramel sauce.

¾ cup sugar

¼ cup water

½ cup heavy cream

3 tablespoons dark rum (optional)

1. Combine the sugar and water in a heavy small saucepan. Bring the pot to a boil and continue to boil the mixture until it turns a light amber color. Do not stir. If part of the syrup is turning darker than the rest of the syrup, gently tilt the pan to even out the cooking.

2. When the syrup is a uniform amber color, stir in the heavy cream with a long-handled wooden spoon. Be careful, because the cream will bubble up. When the bubbling has subsided, stir in the rum, if you are using it. Transfer the sauce to a heat-proof glass measuring cup and let the sauce cool slightly before serving. Caramel Sauce will keep in an airtight container at room temperature for up to 1 week. Reheat the sauce in a microwave for 1½ minutes or on the stovetop before serving.

Maple Walnut Sauce

Makes about 1 cup, enough to accompany 1 pie

This sauce is terrific served over any kind of ice cream and absolutely amazing when poured over slices of Pumpkin Mousse Pie (page 27) or Frozen Cranberry Mousse Pie (page 42).

½ cup pure maple syrup

¼ cup firmly packed dark brown sugar

1 tablespoon unsalted butter

¼ teaspoon salt

½ cup heavy cream

½ cup walnuts, coarsely chopped

1. Combine the maple syrup, brown sugar, butter, and salt in a heavy small saucepan and heat the mixture over medium heat, stirring occasionally, until the sugar is dissolved. Add the heavy cream, bring the pot to a boil, and simmer the sauce for 5 minutes.

2. Remove the pot from the heat and stir in the nuts. Maple Walnut Sauce will keep, refrigerated in an airtight container, for up to 1 week. Reheat the sauce in the microwave for 1½ minutes or on the stovetop before serving.

Berry Mash

Makes about 3 cups, enough to accompany 1 pie

Fresh berries that have been sweetened with sugar are a welcome addition to many icebox pies and also are great on vanilla ice cream. Mash some, but not all, of the berries to help dissolve the sugar and turn the fruit into a sauce.

1 pint fresh raspberries or blueberries, picked over for stems, or strawberries, hulled and sliced

¼ cup sugar, or more to taste

Combine the berries and sugar in a medium-size mixing bowl and stir, mashing about half of the berries with the back of a spoon and leaving the remaining berries intact. Let the berries stand, stirring occasionally, until the sugar is dissolved. Berry Mash will keep, covered with plastic wrap and refrigerated, for up to 6 hours. Let the mash come to room temperature before serving it alongside slices of pie.

Cranberry Dessert Sauce

Makes about 1 cup, enough to accompany 1 pie

This is a good alternative to Berry Mash in winter when good fresh berries are scarce.

½ cup sugar

½ cup orange juice

¾ cup fresh or frozen cranberries, picked over for stems

1 tablespoon orange liqueur

1. Combine the sugar, orange juice, and cranberries in a medium-size saucepan and bring the pot to a boil. Reduce the heat to medium-low and simmer the mixture until the sugar is dissolved, the cranberries have begun to fall apart, and the sauce is thickened, about 5 to 7 minutes.

2. Remove the pot from the heat, stir in the liqueur, and let the sauce cool completely. Serve the sauce cold. Cranberry Dessert Sauce will keep, refrigerated in an airtight container, for up to 1 week.

Raspberry Coulis

Makes about 1 cup, enough to accompany 1 pie

Raspberry Coulis adds color and flavor to many icebox pies.

One 12-ounce bag frozen raspberries, thawed

¼ cup confectioners' sugar, or more to taste

1 tablespoon fresh lemon juice, or more to taste

1. Place the raspberries in a blender or the workbowl of a food processor and process them until they are smooth.

2. Push the purée through a fine mesh strainer to remove the seeds. Stir in the sugar and lemon juice to taste. Raspberry Coulis will keep, refrigerated in an airtight container, for up to 3 days, or in the freezer for up to 6 months.

Mango Coulis

Makes about 1 cup, enough to accompany 1 pie

Use this bright orange sauce as you would use Raspberry Coulis—to add color and acidic flavor to icebox pie.

One 14-ounce bag frozen mango purée, thawed

2 tablespoons confectioners' sugar, or more to taste

1 tablespoon fresh lime juice, or more to taste

Push the mango purée through a fine mesh strainer to remove any strings or tough fibers. Stir in the sugar and lime juice to taste. Mango Coulis will keep, refrigerated in an airtight container, for up to 3 days, or in the freezer for up to 6 months.

Sugared Nuts

Makes ¾ cup

Here's a simple way to sweeten and
toast any kind of nuts.

¾ cup walnut pieces, pecans, whole almonds, pistachio nuts, or skinned hazelnuts (page 50)

2 tablespoons heavy cream

2 tablespoons sugar

¼ teaspoon salt

1. Preheat the oven to 350 degrees.

2. Combine the nuts, heavy cream, sugar, and salt in a small mixing bowl. Turn the mixture onto a baking sheet and bake the nuts until they are golden, 6 to 8 minutes. Let them cool completely. Sugared Nuts will keep in an airtight container at room temperature for up to 1 week.

Nougatine

Makes about ¾ pound

This simple almond brittle is wonderful on its
own or crushed in the food processor and
sprinkled over slices of pie.

1 cup sugar

¼ cup water

1¼ cup sliced almonds

1. Line an 8-inch square baking pan with aluminum foil. Spray a large stainless-steel spoon with nonstick cooking spray.

2. Combine the sugar and water in a heavy medium-size saucepan. Bring the mixture to a boil and cook it without stirring until the mixture turns a light amber color. If part of the syrup is turning darker than the rest of the syrup, gently tilt the pan to even out the cooking.

3. As soon as the syrup is a uniform amber color, stir in the almonds using the greased spoon. Spread the mixture into the foil-lined baking pan and let it cool completely.

4. When the brittle has hardened, peel it from the foil and chop it into small pieces with a chef's knife, or place the brittle in the workbowl of a food processor and process it until it is finely chopped. Nougatine will keep in an airtight container at room temperature for several weeks.

Index